SUNIL BHASKARAN

More Money, More Time, Less Stress

Laser Focus your Mind & Sky Rocket Your
Results while Maintaining Balance

"This time, like all times, is a very good one, if we but know what to do with it."

- Ralph Waldo Emerson

"When people restrain themselves out of fear, their lives are by necessity diminished. Only through freely chosen discipline can life be enjoyed and still kept within the bounds of reason."

- Dr. Mihalyi Csikszentmihalyi, World's Leading Researcher on Positive Psychology, author of 120 articles and book chapters

"Time is the enemy of the poor business and the friend of the great business. If you have a business that's earning 20%-25% on equity, time is your friend. But time is your enemy if your money is in a low return business."

- Warren Buffett, Investor, CEO of Berkshire-Hathaway

"You've got to learn your instrument. Then, you practice, practice, practice. And then, when you finally get up there on the bandstand, forget all that and just wail."

- Charlie "Bird" Parker was an American jazz saxophonist - widely considered one of the most influential of jazz musicians.

Dedicated to my wife Glenda -
The love you give me is worth more than money or time.
I am ever grateful for your love, your supreme creative powers, your elevated listening and our shared humor.
Love,
Sunil

TABLE OF CONTENTS

Introduction

Congratulations!

I wish to acknowledge you for taking a great step in purchasing and reading this book for the following reasons:

- You are in a rare group of people who read to improve themselves

Very few people read to improve themselves consistently. If you live in America, only one in four Americans read a book last year. Most Americans read about 4-5 books a year - most of these books are half or partially finished.[1]

- Your reading this book and applying the principles contained with consistent practice will probably increase your economic success

"Regular reading not only boosts the likelihood of an individual's academic and economic success—facts that are not especially surprising—but it also seems to awaken a person's social and civic sense." -- Research Report by the National Endowment for the Arts[ii]

- Your reading this book and applying the principles contained with consistent practice, will probably reduce your stress

"Overall, people seem to recognize that stress can have an impact on health and well-being, but they do not necessarily take action to prevent stress or manage it well. Survey findings also suggest that time management may be a significant barrier preventing people from taking the necessary steps to improve their health." -- "Stress in America: Our Health at Risk" American Psychological Association[iii]

In this book, you will learn to use strategies to optimize your time usage and productivity, reduce your stress and to put more money in your pocket.

- Your reading this book and applying the principles contained with consistent practice, will probably enable you to have more free or 'choice' time

The majority of people in the United States (and I suspect in other countries now) expect to work more than 40 hours a week. In fact for the majority of people who work, it is considered 'career suicide' to work anything less than 40 hours a week. For some solo-preneurs, entrepreneurs and professionals, 40 hours a week

Sunil Bhaskaran

is considered part time – the expectations for weekly hours is in the realm of 60 hours and up, including work on the weekends.

This book gives an opportunity for you to look at work, wealth, business and life in a different way – a way that will enable you to have More Money, More Time... and Less Stress.

How this training helped me create More Money & More TIME & Less Stress

I truly enjoy my life and work. I am not unlike you in the sense that, from time to time I feel dejected, resigned, frustrated, guilt-ridden and a little scared. However, there are four ways that I am different from most people:

- I don't stay hooked or reactivated by these feelings for too long

- I differentiate between enjoyment and pleasure and this differentiation has freed me up in my attitude and overall way of being in life

- I embrace challenges and victories as a path to enjoyment

- I learned to focus and this skill gives me infinite enjoyment and increasing amounts of money yearly

It took practice on my part, to get to this state of being. I believe, with practice, that you can achieve this way of being as well.

There is a difference between enjoyment and pleasure for me:[iv] Enjoyment for me involves embracing the hard challenges as well as the sweet victories – I embrace both. Pleasure tends to come from avoiding challenges, and in having nice experiences.

I assert that learning to enjoy gives one a more sustainable balance in life and work. It gives more sustainable and desirable results (e.g. money, health, relationships, etc.) over time and also increases moments of nice, pleasant experiences.

The path to enjoying life is to learn to manage your distractions. I find that the more I am able to manage my distractions and stay focused, the more I infinitely enjoy life – and I do mean infinitely enjoy life.

The distractions act like a Three Stooges comedy – endlessly flip flopping from one skit to another – it becomes more and more difficult to settle on one thought or act or experience. Very often the distracting thoughts prevent one from experiencing the myriad of rich inputs that your sensory systems in your brain are receiving at any one point.

I pause now to sense what is the richness of my current experience as I write these words – there is a beautiful fog over Monterey Bay, California of which I have a view – it fills me with serenity and vulnerability. I feel my body seated cozily in my track suit – this fills with me with gratitude for a wonderful life. I have a thought about my dear wife, Glenda and my heart slows down in its beating – I can feel this change. I take a deep wonderful breath and feel my lungs filling up with fresh air – and I feel the promise of the rest of my life. Another memory comes to my mind about my dear mother and I feel secure and well taken care of. The list can go on if you allow yourself to be present sequentially and in depth to each experience.

You could ask "Well Sunil, that sounds nice but what is the point of experiencing these sensations sequentially and in depth?"

The point is that for the most part, when you are distracted from your experience of sensations by other thoughts or you flit from one experience to the next without truly appreciating the depth of each experience – you miss out on most of what life can offer you and the depth of each experience.

WHY THIS MAKES A DIFFERENCE IN MAKING MORE MONEY

This richness and depth is what helps people to do the following with regards to earning money and wealth generation:

- Sell your services and products better because you speak from your integrated heart and mind

- Calmly and clearly attract and discern the perfect kinds of people who want to be your customers or clients or friends

- Give you the freedom and insight to create even better services and products to increase your wealth – creating the future that you want including vacations for your family, time and money to do the things you truly enjoy, and fulfilling the bigger dreams that have seemed elusive till now.

When I first started my business, I went from zero clients to a full clientele (22 clients at that time) within one week. I accomplished this primarily because I did more than 200 interactions per day (over email and phone or speaking to a group) to generate business. I only counted an interaction if I asked for business, an appointment or a referral. I made my goal of a full practice in one week – however I was burnt out.

It took a while and a lot of maturing in sophistication, but I finally cracked the code of generating business while maintaining a healthy lifestyle. The 2 really do go together – living a healthy lifestyle and generating a business/career.

I still remember the time when my wife and I were on Maui (Hawaii) on the top of a very high volcano scanning the view of the nearby islands and the Pacific Ocean – I knew that in that moment, my team and my admin at home were busy working on my business and taking care of my clients. I asked myself "What would someone have to pay me to give up this beautiful experience?" I went up to about $10 million dollars before I could say I would be willing to give up this experience – and even then I had my doubts.

After all, what is the point of generating business and money if you can't live a full life?

In the pages that follow, I will share with you how you can get More Time, More Money and Less Stress... and have the quality of life that you deserve.

Enjoy,

Sunil Bhaskaran

How to Use this Book - Recommendations

One of the things that I noticed about people who do any kind of learning or reading, is that they are initially very inspired to get into action (typically right after or while reading the book) but then the distractions of their life creep in or rush in and they end up achieving nothing.

There are 3 recommendations that I have:

Pace yourself in reading this book. You don't have to get everything done in one day - that may be counter-productive. Pace yourself and give yourself some time each day or every few days to read this book and then schedule times to do the practices and actions.

Make sure that you practice what I suggest: the brain only responds to actions. No action implies very little change in your brain. With action, your brain responds and creates new neural pathways representing new habits and new ways of thinking[v]. You will even feel a greater sense of enjoyment.

Come with an open mind. Be open to the ideas here especially if you think that you may have heard them before. You may have done other trainings in the past. I am not asking you to give up what you learned before, but to consider what you are about to read as brand new information. That sense of newness will give your brain a chance to absorb and truly learn.

If you are an Employee

This training is very relevant to you as an employee. Although some of the concepts presented here are directed at entrepreneurs, you will find the concepts very valuable and applicable to your work in a company. The invitation is for you to think like an entrepreneur – someone who is up to having things work for herself (or himself) as well as for other people involved. The advantages to this approach are that you will learn how to think creatively and still make your work in your company productive and joyful.

THE SCIENTIFIC BACKGROUND

I realize that some of you may not want to read through much scientific data. I have tried to limit the amount of data that I present and also to present the data in a simplified manner. I have included an End Notes section at the end of the book that contains references to other texts and research data for those who want more details.

Brain science is a rapidly advancing field. In 2007 alone, there were at least 3 studies coming out every hour. We invite you to connect with us on our website (www.CahayaMind.com) and our social media to stay abreast of this new technology.

Sunil Bhaskaran

A Summary of the Sections contained in this book

Section One: Building Awareness: Understanding Yourself, Your Mind, Your Time and Your Money

This section builds up your awareness of your brain, time and money. This awareness leads us to breakthroughs in our productivity. You could say that any consciously created breakthrough begins with a level of awareness. Without awareness, your successes and breakthroughs are dependent on luck or other external factors. Directed breakthroughs require a degree of awareness.

Section Two: Build Your Future: Creating a Brand New Context for Your Time, Money and reduced stress.

In this critical section, I help you create a powerful reason for making the changes that you need, to help you move forward. Without this reason or context, it becomes easy to be distracted from your mission to fulfill your goals, dreams and future. I also include practices that are designed to get you into action.

PROACTIVITY

At appropriate points in the text, you will get the following to solidify your learning process:

- The takeaways or summary of main points in the sub-section

- Space for you to take notes

- Assignments to help you deepen your knowledge from that sub section

- Case Studies of Actual Clients pertinent to the content

Section One: Understanding Yourself, Your Mind, Your Time and Your Money

Sunil Bhaskaran

RELATIONSHIP BETWEEN TIME AND MONEY – AN INTRODUCTION TO OUTCOME BASED THINKING

We want to start by distinguishing between an outcome and a task.

So what is an outcome and what is a task?

OUTCOME: An outcome is a desired result to be achieved within a specified timeline that can be measured as follows:

A measure (number or observable event or experience associated with an outcome/action) that adds up to something meaningful or intended in the long term.

Example of a number measure: "I will make $56 in income today"

Example of an observable event: "I will have the report on your desk by the end of today"

Example of an experience "I feel fulfilled by the end of today in spending time with my spouse"

This number, observable event or experience associated with an outcome/action is pertinent to your mission (or vision) and your long term goals: this is important as I want you to train yourself to focus on making your daily, weekly, monthly and yearly outcomes add up to the longer term vision, mission and goals.

TASK: A task on the other hand is more action oriented: something that you do to make the outcome happen – but it is not the ultimate outcome desired e.g. "I will make 5 calls today" on the surface looks like an outcome: but notice that it is more about activity (i.e. making calls) than it is about outcomes that are desired (e.g. making a sale, making an appointment, getting a referral, getting a speaking engagement).

Examples of outcomes are your goals and promises. Outcomes could be defined over a period of a specified number of minutes to a specified number of years i.e. the deadline date for the delivery of these outcomes could extend from a specified number of minutes to a specified number of years.

Here are some surprising things that I have found out about the relationship between time and money. The following is an observation from more than 20 years of coaching businesses and professionals as well as running my own business.

- **If you commit to spending less time on tasks, you tend to make more money.** When people commit to spending more energy and time to generating relevant outcomes – outcomes that are relevant to their business, they make more money. The key word in the previous statement is 'commit' – you have to be willing to interrupt current behaviors and habits to make this shift. I have seen this particularly in clients who have a life threatening disease or some other crisis that prevents them from working too many hours – they (with few exceptions with extenuating circumstances) find a way to make the same or more money (usually more money) in less time. Where there is a commitment, there is usually a solution.

THE DIFFERENCE BETWEEN AN OUTCOME AND A TASK

The keyword is 'outcome'. If you focus on outcomes rather than tasks, then you are more likely to produce results (outcomes) rather than a history of work that you carried out. Outcomes are what counts and outcomes don't lie. You either have the outcomes or the history of tasks that you carried out.

People have a difficult time initially distinguishing between an outcome and a task: this is normal for most people to experience – so if you find yourself being a little challenged in trying to distinguish between the two, know that you are not alone. However, with time, you can begin to distinguish these more clearly.

We want you as the reader to get accustomed to this new way of thinking. With every new way of thinking comes a new language e.g. when medical students learn about the body, they learn a new language (many medical terms are based in Latin). The new language gives more proficiency in the new way of thinking. To have you ingrain this new way of thinking, we will be using the term 'outcome' throughout the rest of this book rather than goals.

The more awareness you bring to your time usage, the more money you are likely to make. Awareness is the first key to change or transformation. If you have tried to make more money in less time in the past and have failed, do not fear – you can make a shift, change or transformation by firstly becoming more aware.

CASE HISTORY: MICHAEL[VI]

Michael runs a very successful software business. He kept complaining before he met me about being at the end of the week, and feeling like he had not accomplished anything at all. At that time, he was making about $300k per year. He started tracking his time to see where he was spending time. He was shocked to see how much time he was spending on "research on the internet". This was with the intention of discovering more about his market – however, he was spending a lot of that time on distracting websites that had a very peripheral connection to what he was really looking for. On hindsight, this was obvious but not obvious when he was caught up in the middle of the work. With this insight, he started shifting more time towards researching in limited time periods of 10 minutes or less and on much focused research outcomes – he did the same with about 10 other areas of time usage. Within one year, his income shot up to $500,000.00 – there were many reasons for this income growth spurt – but certainly effective time usage was one of the primary factors. The lessons persisted and four years later, his annual income shot to over $5 million.

Sunil Bhaskaran

Takeaways:

- If you commit to spending less time on tasks and more time on outcomes, you make more money.

- The more awareness you bring to your time usage, the more likely for you to make more money in less time

- Please review the definition above of an outcome

Get into Action:

Schedule a period of time this week where you will track your time usage. Track your time usage for at least 3 business days. Then review the data while asking the following questions:

Where are you spending too much time?

In these areas, are you producing enough outcomes that give you money or satisfaction?

If you expect outcomes from doing these tasks, when do you realistically expect these outcomes to occur in a satisfactory manner?

Do you have a logical basis for justifying your answers?

What lessons have you learned from this exercise?

What actions will you take from now on to resolve what you have learned?

NOTES:

OPTIMIZE YOUR BRAIN FUNCTION, OPTIMIZE YOUR EFFECTIVENESS

Your brain pretty much dictates (in cooperation with your body) your effectiveness. This may seem like a cliché. The problem with clichés is that they are mostly true and horribly ignored. If your brain function is not optimized, your performance is not optimized.

In the last five years, we have discovered more about the brain than in the last 100 years of brain research. We have expanded the reach of brain science into areas pertaining to the unconscious, day to day work performance, decision making, sources of morality, emotional regulation and more.

Everything you experience and do begins and ends with the brain. Everything you see, touch, feel or hear is ultimately processed in the brain for you to have an experience. Everything you affect in your environment (e.g. moving the table to the side of the room e.g. talking with your daughter about her new boyfriend, etc.) is sourced ultimately in your brain. On top of this, consider that when you speak or interact with others, you are fundamentally responding to and interacting with their nervous systems as well.

Sunil Bhaskaran

Fantasy Time Management

I call the following narrative Fantasy Time Management.

"I wake up early in the morning fresh from a great sleep at 5 am. I play two rounds of golf and then get to work on time after eating a healthy, hearty breakfast. I get to work and make 9,000 phone calls before lunch. I have a great networking lunch from 12 noon to 1 pm and appear back at work at 1.15 pm sharp. I then make another 7,000 calls before 5 pm: end work at 5 pm and go back home where my spouse waits patiently for me. I have a quiet dinner with my spouse and children and then read my novel before retiring peacefully at 9.00 pm to bed, to get another fresh 8 hours of sleep"

I think you get my point -even if I vastly exaggerate to make the point clear. Most people have an unrealistic assessment of their time, their abilities to get stuff done and the possibility of unexpected events and distractions.[vii]

Takeaway:

We tend to have our time management based on a fantasy of what we can achieve in a day rather than based in reality.

Get into Action:

Identify areas of your life, work or business where you have unrealistic expectations of your time management or willpower to get things done.

Ask yourself the following questions

What are the unrealistic expectations that I have for the day, week, month and year?

For the expectations that I think are realistic, what makes me think that they are realistic?

What are some of the realistic expectations that you have that have not been fulfilled for .. perhaps too long?

NOTES:

FINDING QUALITY OF LIFE IN THE MIDST OF BUSINESS AND PRODUCTIVITY

As technology has improved with smart phones, mobile devices, the internet, social media etc., we have become more connected electronically – you can reach about 5.6 billion people in the world today via mobile technology and the internet[viii]: However, we have also lost a sense of privacy, intimacy, depth and solitude which some of us really do value above being "connected all the time".

Here is a quote from "Hamlet's Blackberry" by William Powers[ix]

"Now and then it occurs to us that we could do better, reconfigure our commitments and schedules so they're not so crazy and we can breathe. But no sooner do we have this thought than we dismiss it as futile. The mad rush is the real world, we tell ourselves. We're resigned to it in the same grim way that people in repressive societies become resigned to their lack of freedom."

Get into Action:

Where in your life, does the "mad rush of the world" occur in your life?

How does it impact you and people around you?

NOTES:

Sunil Bhaskaran

The Myth of Multitasking and Multitasking effectiveness

There is no such thing as multi-tasking as far as the brain is concerned for most of your day to day tasks[x]. For most day to day tasks, the brain does task switching: it switches from one task to another. You might ask me "Well… then how do we eat a sandwich and drive at the same time?" Mechanical activities like driving usually are learned in a part of the brain that is different from the part of the brain involved in day to day work – however these activities take a lot of time and practice to become automatic or effortless.

For most of your day to day tasks, the brain is not multitasking. Every time you switch from one task to another, the brain goes through 4 sequential steps[xi] that have to be done in sequence. These 4 steps take time and energy and have to be done sequentially – hence there is no multitasking that occurs in the brain and our attempts to multi-task does take some energy. The brain shuts down or slows down when it detects a lowering of available energy due to the multitasking occurring.[xii]

Yet people attempt to multitask all the time. You may see yourself checking your social media page, your email, your project status – some people have 5, 6, 10 windows open on their computers at any point, moving from one window to another in rapid succession.

'Multitasking' is a very energy-expensive thing to do and reduces your effectiveness, reliability, health and your abilities to make money considerably. Not to mention the effect on your relationships when you try to check your social media page whilst talking with your spouse and sending a text message to your child who is being reprimanded by his teacher.

Multi-tasking is, for all intents and purposes, a self-imposed series of interruptions or distractions.

Studies show that a person who is interrupted takes 50 percent longer to finish a task. They also make up to 50 percent more errors.[xiii]

Some of you may be good at multi-tasking in certain situations: you probably have learned to have certain tasks be more automatic and can do these tasks with little 'brain energy drain' – however this level of training takes at least a few months if not years to accomplish (e.g. how long did it take before you could eat a sandwich and drive at the same time?). The point is that you may be able to multi task with tasks that you are conditioned to be automatic with; but with newer skills, competencies, more complex projects and practices, you may be better off not multi-tasking, at least for the short term.

I want to train you to reduce your multitasking habits and create more focus and depth in your life, work and relationships.

NOTES:

CASE STUDY: BILL (COMMERCIAL REALTOR)

When Bill first came to me, his ADHD (Attention Deficit Hyperactive Disorder)[xiv] was clear – he was late to the appointment with me and had come in flustered and angry at himself for being distracted by things that really did not matter to him, but he felt were important in the moment they came up.

"How do you gauge what is important and what to focus on?" he asked me looking very sad and hopeless. "Everything seems so important… especially in the world of commercial real estate…"

"What would you like to see happen?" I asked.

He hesitated and finally answered "To make my income targets primarily… then to make sure that I have a viable sustainable flow of clients… and to have at least a few hours a week with my family… and to … lose 10 lbs.…"

This was the beginning of his ascent to being a multi-million dollar producer in real estate. Once you identify where you want to go clearly and what is the highest priority, the brain has a better chance of putting together a plan and actions to take you exactly there.

It took a while for Bill to change his habits of doing many things at the same time. Understandably, there is a push in the world today to do many things at once – but over time, Bill learned to do the following

a. Identify what his primary outcomes were daily, and focus more time on these

b. As he mastered a. above, he started to learn to plan longer term on a smaller set of outcomes for the month and then the year and then 5 years out

c. As he mastered b. above and started to make more luxurious cash-flow, he learned to plan even longer for 10 years out

In other words, he became better at focusing on few outcomes over time – enabling the best of his energies to be devoted to what was most important.

Takeaway:

For the most part, the brain does not multitask – it does task switching i.e. switching from one task to another. The experience of multitasking leads to energy depletion and a shutting down of the brain.

Get into Action:

Start noticing and writing down the costs of multitasking in your life: the impacts on your family, friends, your health, your ability to earn income, your abilities to manage your finances, etc.

NOTES:

THE MYTH OF THE EFFECTIVENESS OF THE TO-DO LIST

The majority of my clients have long to-do lists when they first come to me. These to-do lists typically are long and contain items from the dawn of time. I exaggerate but it is quite true that people have items on this list that are outdated or old.

The problem with relying on to-do lists is as follows:

You have to keep checking the to-do list to see what you could do next. This is an activity that takes up brain power in itself. This is very different from what I suggest in this book - where you need not bother remembering to look at something: rather you are reminded by an external agent: e.g. an alarm from a reminder. Hence you eliminate the worrying need to continually check your to-do list and instead let the sounded alarm guide you to do what is next.

You double your work when you have a to-do list: looking at the list, you always have to weigh what to do next. Your brain can actually contain on an average, in its working memory about 7 items at any time, so if you have a list of more than 7, this can put a strain on available brain resources.

I want to train you to move away from your to-do list in a respectful and comfortable manner to a more efficient manner of managing your time and promised outcomes.

Takeaway:

The to-do list is an inefficient way to get things done. A temporary to do list – one which gets cleared out by the end of the day is more workable.

Get into Action:

How old is each item on your current to-do list?

Is the to-do list serving you? How exactly?

What does it cost you to manage the to-do list? E.g. stress, time, money?

NOTES:

DISTRACTIONS

Many of my clients when they first start working with me complain about numerous kinds of distractions: everything from being distracted by their kids to incessant and negative self-talk to exciting news in their business to thoughts of what they should be doing instead of what they have in front of them now.

Some people are addicted to certain kinds of distractions e.g. watching TV, surfing the internet, checking emails, social media, food, alcohol, drugs, etc. The list of potential distractions could go on for a long time.

These distractions can stem from addictions. The world of addiction and the world of distractions are not distantly related.

Addictions stem from a wonderful chemical in your brain called dopamine. There are other bio-chemicals involved and dopamine plays a big part in this game. Dopamine is a reward-based chemical: it gives you that pleasant feeling when you know that you are on track for some kind of reward e.g. if you are hunting for fruit and you see something bright orange in the forest, you know that you may be on track for eating oranges – this system helps you stay on track to the oranges – this reward system evolved to help you survive.

You can replace the orange color with almost anything that is attractive to most of us e.g. a potential mate, the promise of sex, lovely colors, enticing dancing, the look of an ice-cold beer, the color of the wrapping around your favorite brand of chocolate, etc.

As you equate distractions with things that you like to do e.g. time on your Facebook, watching videos online, your dopamine levels tend to go up even when you think about Facebook or watching a video.

Get into Action:

Attempt to focus on a task for the next one minute. Keep track of how many times you get distracted in the next one minute (set an alarm for one minute).

Now do the same exercise for the next five minutes, then the next 10 minutes.

As you think of something that you like to do and that also distracts you, what are the feelings that you experience in just thinking about these activities?

What did you learn?

NOTES:

Sunil Bhaskaran

CREATING FLOW IN YOUR LIFE

Dr. Mihaly Csikszentmihalyi (pronounced *MEE-hy CHEEK-sent-ma-HY-ee*) has researched what is called the flow (or optimal state of inner experience) as well as happiness and creativity for at least the last 35 years. He has written 120 articles or book chapters on positive psychology and is referred to as the world's leading researcher on positive psychology.

He said "The optimal state of inner experience is one in which there is order in consciousness. This happens when psychic energy – or attention – is invested in realistic goals, and skills match the opportunities"[xv]

This is a primary desire for many people - They have experienced an optimal state of inner experience from time to time and desire to have more of it.

This experience of flow is achieved when your skill levels just match or are slightly lower than your challenge levels in a particular domain. E.g. in the domain of marketing in your business, if your challenge level is only a little bit beyond your skill levels, chances are that you will be only slightly challenged overall and be in an excited or motivated state.

The following are the cases for most people

- Your skill level is very low and your challenge is very high: you will probably feel a great deal of anxiety e.g. in driving, if your skills are not very good and you feel challenged when driving in the middle of a very crowded and unruly city where people don't follow the rules, then you may feel very anxious.

- Your skill level is very high and your challenge is very low: you will probably feel bored.

- Your skill level is matching or just lower than your challenge level: you are in a positive or flow state

If you know where you are at in your current state, you can start gradually increasing your skill or challenge (or reducing challenge depending on the situation) to achieve flow state.

Get into Action:

List out your main domains of interest e.g. relationship with your spouse e.g. marketing your business e.g. managing your time e.g. leadership e.g. managing your team etc.

For each of these main domains, indicate what level of challenge and what level of skill you have in each domain (very skilled = 10, zero to low skill =0, very challenged = 10, low challenge = 0)

Notice what emotional state you have for each domain (Anxious, bored/relaxed, apathy or flow)

What steps can you take in modifying either your skill state (e.g. upgrading or more education) or moderating your challenge level (e.g. cutting down on the expectations of the project) to moderate your stress and increase your flow and productivity?

NOTES:

Sunil Bhaskaran

Building Your Willpower

From the latest research on willpower[xvi], we now know that willpower is a finite resource in all of us. There is a biological limit. This well of willpower in your nervous system is dictated by the availability of glucose[xvii] to your brain and your ability to use the glucose. This glucose is derived from the food that you eat. However, obviously you cannot keep eating in order to build up willpower as that causes all kinds of other problems e.g. diabetes, heart problems etc.

Every time you make a decision or switch from one task to another or use willpower to focus and stick to a task, it takes up energy or glucose – your glucose levels in your blood stream literally drop. This causes you to act irrationally or to make bad decisions or to become far less disciplined.[xviii]

The fact of the matter is that willpower for the most part is like a finite bank account: however most of us operate like it is an infinite bank account. This results in an unrealistic assessment of what can be done in one day. This also results in mismanagement of promised outcomes: over promising, under delivering.

I am not saying that you cannot increase your willpower – I am saying the opposite. You can build up your willpower over time.

When you have a finite or limited bank account as is in the case of will-power, there are three things to do

- Make sure that your account does not run dry

- Make sure that whatever you spend in your account gives you a good return on your investment

And perhaps of most interest,

- Continue to build reserves so that you can over time, stretch the availability and application of your willpower i.e. start stretching your abilities and willpower

You expend willpower every time you do one or more of the following

- Resist temptations or distractions

- Work through obstacles to get to an outcome or resolution of a problem

As willpower is expended in these ways on the path to an outcome, it would make sense to get clear on your outcomes – I would hate to see you spend all that energy, moving towards an outcome, only to find out that what you achieved was not quite what you wanted in the first place.

I see this happen time and time again in working with some people – they create a desired outcome that is nebulous or unclear – and they end up having an outcome that was not at all what they wanted in the first place. If only they had been clear?

What I have seen personally in my career as a mentor to many business and professional people is that there are three primary reasons why desired outcomes are not achieved:

- The outcomes were unclear or not clear enough

- The outcomes were conflicting with either their values or conflicting within the set of outcomes i.e. one outcome conflicted with another outcome

- They don't learn to manage their distractions and learn how to focus

Get into Action:

Identify clearly what your desired outcomes are
Identify as best as you can any conflicts between these outcomes
Identify any belief systems that impede you in achieving these outcomes

NOTES:

Sunil Bhaskaran

Outcomes and Belief systems

The main reasons why people fail to reach outcomes are

Two or more of their outcomes or beliefs conflict with each other[xix] e.g. I want to make more money ($10k this month) AND I want to spend 40 hours more with my family this month. I believe that in order to make more money, I have to spend less time with my family: hence there is a conflict. This literally results in a person being torn between two outcomes and unable to focus entirely on either.

The outcomes are unclear e.g. I want to be more confident. This is unclear and very difficult to measure or to observe accurately.

They **don't learn to manage their distractions** and learn how to focus

NOTES:

TAKE CARE OF YOUR **PFC** – THE PART OF YOUR BRAIN THAT YOU USE MOST DAILY!

The part of your brain that is most used in day to day work is called the Prefrontal Cortex (PFC). This is located right behind your forehead area. It plays a big part in decision making, understanding, memory retention, emotional regulation, task switching, recalling memories and many other functions. It is the part of the brain that is most connected to other parts of the brain especially to the parts of the brain that generate impulses (distractions, stress responses, fear responses, disgust responses, guilt, frustration, resignation, etc.): the prefrontal cortex plays a large role in managing and mitigating your impulses.

However, the prefrontal cortex is a very inefficient part of your brain - Inefficient in two ways:

- Energy inefficient

- Memory inefficient

It is energy inefficient because it takes up a lot of energy to get things done. The brain itself takes up about 20 percent of your caloric (food) intake. It has been shown in the laboratory that every time you make a decision or switch from one task to another (all functions of the prefrontal cortex), the glucose level in your blood stream goes down[xx]. Glucose gets converted into neurotransmitters in your brain – neurotransmitters enable your brain to work: less neurotransmitters implies that your brain begins to shut down or slow down. Thus if you overload the prefrontal cortex with too much work, your brain stops working effectively and efficiently.

It is memory inefficient in that it has a very small working memory associated with it. Imagine if you had a computer with very limited memory e.g. memory that could only store one small file as opposed too many files. It would be very difficult today to use a computer like that: the computer would be very slow in processing things.

Takeaway:

The prefrontal cortex while still fairly quick and effective has limitations on what it can work with at any one time. Overload the prefrontal cortex with tasks and you start getting diminishing outcomes and reduced abilities to manage stress, resignation, guilt, distractions etc.

NOTES:

DOPAMINE: REWARDS, OUTCOMES, MOTIVATION

How people manage their expectations relative to their ability to produce the outcomes that they want is critical.

Dopamine is a wonderful naturally occurring chemical in your brain. It is a neurotransmitter and is commonly associated with the reward system, providing feelings of enjoyment as well as motivation.[xi] It has been shown in scientific research that every time you have a failed expectation, your dopamine levels go down.[xxii] The converse is true: if you meet expectations, your dopamine levels go up. This provides motivation to go on and do more.

One way we mismanage our expectations is in how we select and manage the outcomes in our business and in our life. If we set up outcomes that are unrealistic, we set ourselves up to fight against our dopamine based biology.

It behooves us to manage our outcomes on a daily basis: to be realistic about our expectations. The more realistic our outcomes and the more we manage them, the more likely we are to create fulfilled expectations and thus greater levels of motivation – what I call an upward spiral of confidence and motivation. If we don't manage our outcomes well, and have unrealistic expectations about our abilities, which is how most people conduct their busy lives, then we are more likely to end up with decreased levels of motivation – what I call a downward spiral.

While this mechanism is partly responsible for addictive behaviors, in responsibly managed situations it can result in better productivity without the undue effects of stress and overwork.

Takeaway:

Managing your expectations or outcomes will help you manage your motivation levels. Creating unrealistic outcomes that are consistently not met, results in lower levels of motivation. Creating realistic outcomes that are met more often, results in higher levels of motivation.

Questions:

What are your primary outcomes for this year?
What are your primary outcomes for this month?
What are your primary outcomes for this week?
What are your primary outcomes for today?
Which of these outcomes are realistic? Which are not?
Why?

NOTES:

MANAGING IMPULSES AND DISTRACTIONS

There are parts of the brain that are responsible for generating distraction and responding to impulses. Nature gave us these impulses and distractions to help us survive in the times of our ancestors who lived in day to day, if not minute to minute survival. However, these impulses and distractions remain a part of our brain biology today despite a much reduced need to survive daily and minute to minute.

The prefrontal cortex part of your brain helps in inhibiting or 'braking' these impulses and distractions. However, as we described in the previous section, the prefrontal cortex is also energy inefficient; the more stress you put on the prefrontal cortex, the less likely you are to be efficiently inhibiting or 'braking' these impulses and distractions.

Takeaway:

It behooves us to learn how to strengthen habits that enable the appropriate inhibition of these impulses and distractions so that we can be more productive.

Questions

What are 20 typical distractions for you?

What are the top 5 distractions?

What would your life be like if you had less of these distractions or if these distractions had less of a 'hold' or effect on you?

NOTES:

Sunil Bhaskaran

Increase Your Creativity

More than 50 percent of the workers today do creative work.[xxiii]

In today's information based world, creative people are finding ways to represent information in novel ways. Novelty begets attention. If you get attention, you sell products and services.

To get to novelty, you have to create insight which requires different kinds of thinking than most of us are accustomed to.

But most of us get to a point of impasse – where we feel stuck and fail to get to insight because we essentially are stuck in thinking a particular way.

Based on the latest research on impasse resolution in brain science, it has been found that the prefrontal cortex or the part of the brain that is most active during the workday is the main obstacle in the way of getting to insights or new kinds of thinking.

When I ask people at my seminars, when they usually get insights, most of the answers I receive are of the form "In the shower", "While taking a walk", "While I meditated", "I took a break", "In the hot tub", "I bent over to tie my shoelace and I saw the entire solution" etc.

It seems like you have to almost step outside of your usual prefrontal cortex centered mode of operating: understanding, recalling memories, deciding, etc. and allow the subconscious to 'figure it out'.

What I have found is when people do the practices contained in this book, they tend to stress their prefrontal cortex less – this decrease in stress and usage leads ultimately to more insights.

Takeaway:

Put less stress on the Prefrontal cortex and chances are that your creativity, insightfulness and willpower will increase.

Get into Action

Recall the last time that you had an insight

What were you doing at that time?

How often do you create insightful experience for yourself?

What typically gets in the way of creating insightful experience?

If you created more insight, how do you think your life, career or business could improve?

What are the costs of not creating insight in your life?

NOTES:

THE NATURE OF STRESS – UNDERSTANDING STRESS

Stress is one of the biggest killers of human beings. We live in a very complex world today – far more complex than our ancestors ever did. However, our brains have for the most part, not changed much from our ancestors' days.

We have the same brain functions that helped protect our ancestors from prey, hunger, unpredictable climatic changes and other dangers.

Some scientists consider that there are two 'people' metaphorically living inside your brain:[xxiv]

The Impulsive Person: A person who represents our impulses and wants us to respond to our impulses

The Rational Person: A person who represents our ability to control our impulses and do the things that we may not necessarily want to do but know that we need to do

We need both these 'people'. We need to be able to respond to impulses e.g. if you are crossing the road, you want to be able to respond to impulses telling you to avoid an onrushing car. We need the second person as he will tell us not to kill the postman who delivers a large tax bill to you from the Internal Revenue Service.

However, over indulgence with the impulses results in our brains becoming overly active and reactive and ... stressed out.

Both these persons work antagonistically i.e. if one person (e.g. Rational Person) gets strong, the other (e.g. Impulsive Person) tends to get weak.

The impulses (fear, anxiety, etc.) result in the secretion of adrenaline and cortisol into our blood stream. These are useful chemicals when it comes to running away from predators (e.g. a large tiger or lion) – adrenaline gives you a sudden shot of energy you will need to run fast – cortisol kicks in later to help soothe things down.

Of course, today we no longer are threatened by the same kinds of predators or dangers in our day to day life. However, our brains have not changed and respond to perceived threats in the same way. For example, our brain still sends alarm messages to secrete adrenaline and then later cortisol when it senses a movement around you, when your boss shows up at your private meeting, when you sense some other car driver behind you tailgating you, when you see your teen age daughter's Facebook postings, when you are five minutes late to a meeting, when someone disagrees with you, when the phone rings, when people stare at you differently from what you are accustomed, when your banker clears his throat looking through your account information, etc. etc.

These kinds of minute to minute stimuli give more frequent shots of adrenaline and cortisol into your blood stream. Waves of adrenaline and cortisol can wreak havoc in your body. Our bodies were not evolved to handle continuous waves of these two chemicals – our bodies were only designed to handle very occasional stimuli.

Stress creates obesity, heart disease and has been linked to a whole host of other diseases and health problems.

The good news is that when we instigate the Rational Person part of the brain, this tends to calm down the Impulsive Person part of our brains, thus resulting in far less unnecessary stress. The means to doing this is to use the practices in this book collectively including but not limited to better time management tactics, the effective selection of high return outcomes, the selection of realistic outcomes, reducing conflicts between outcomes, etc. The Rational Person can also be 'brought in' by creating and using systems and structures that support you in moving forward e.g. a proper calendar, a calm and objective business mentor or coach, meetings with clear agendas and timelines etc.

Get into action: Questions to increase your awareness:
Recall a time when your impulses ruled the moment
What did it feel like in your body – any sensations in the body? What were your thoughts?
Recall a time when your impulses ruled the moment and then you brought in Rational Person
What changed and how?
What would be possible if your Rational Person was brought in more often?
In what ways (systems, structures, accountability systems etc.) can the Rational Person be brought in more often in your day, week and month?

Takeaway:
You could say that there are two people in your brain: Impulsive and Rational Person. When your impulses get out of control, stress increases. When your Rational Person kicks in, your Impulsive Person shrinks more into the background and stress decreases. When your Impulsive Person kicks in, your Rational Person tends to shrink into the background.

NOTES:

TASKS VERSUS PERFORMANCE: THE MORE YOU DO THE LESS YOU GET BACK!

As you remember the definition of a task:

TASK: A task is more action oriented: something that you do to make the outcome happen – but it is not the ultimate outcome desired e.g. "I will make 5 calls today" on the surface looks like an outcome: but notice that it is more about activity (i.e. making calls) than it is about outcomes that are desired (e.g. making a sale, making an appointment, getting a referral, getting a speaking engagement).

Most of us live in an illusion about performance. We think that as long as we do more, we will get more in return in terms of outcomes.

However, that is only true to a point. Research that goes back to the early 20th century shows that your performance goes up initially as you increase the tasks or the complexity of tasks. You feel the energy coming about because that is how we are designed to respond initially to tasks. As we do more, our performance initially increases due to the initial spurt of energy expended. However, at some point (depending on the complexity of the tasks), any additional complexity or number of tasks added on will only serve to decrease performance.

So as you initially increase your tasks, performance might increase.

But as you add more tasks, at some point, performance starts decreasing and continues to do so.

To picture this graphically in your mind, imagine an Upside down 'U' graph. Performance goes up first and then goes down just like in an upside down or inverted 'U'.

This relationship is expressed as the Yerkes-Dodson Law and applies to your performance relating to your prefrontal cortex. This is not difficult to understand now: the limitations of the prefrontal cortex in terms of energy and memory will naturally provide a limit on how much you can handle at any point.

This limit, I have found from consulting with people on performance, seems to be around 4 to 7 outcomes per day; the number tends more towards 4 than 7 on most days.

The number can go up if you are dealing with less complex tasks and tasks that you have some degree of automaticity in e.g. some people can respond to certain kinds of emails almost mechanically without thinking: these people will find that this task may not count towards much in their abilities to handle more tasks per day.

Takeaway:

Initially when you increase the number and complexity of your tasks, your performance may go up. However, at some point (typically around 4 to 7 tasks) your performance starts going down with each additional task.

Sunil Bhaskaran

Get into action: Questions to increase your awareness:

At any average moment in your day to day work, how many tasks do you think you are doing in that moment?

Over the period of a day, how many tasks are you doing or intend to do?

How many do you actually get done per day?

NOTES:

FLEXIBILITY VS. CHAOS/RIGIDITY

Most people live either in some degree of chaos for the most part OR they live rigidly. They relate to their time management from a place of chaos or from a place of rigidity. In chaos, people have little or no structure, planning or organization. In rigidity, people live and abide strictly by rules or structure to the point of non-effectiveness.

What I advocate is a more flexible approach to managing your outcomes, time and life.

A good analogy would be a tree:

- A chaotic tree that has no structure at all will easily fall down and be washed away in a storm.

- A rigid tree would also fall down easily in a storm.

- A flexible tree can bend and move with the storm and has less chance of being blown or wash away

Being flexible is a good thing for a tree especially in storms. Coconut trees have this ability to bend and withstand the forces of storms.

Questions to ponder:

In your daily time management, do you lean more towards being rigid OR chaotic in your approach to managing your outcomes and work?

You may have certain areas where you are more chaotic in your approach: which areas are these?

You may have other areas where you are more rigid in your approach: which areas are these?

In those areas where you are more chaotic, what would be possible if you brought in a bit more flexibility – combining structure or systems with a willingness to modify the structure or systems as appropriate with the intention of producing outcomes and having things work?

In those areas where you are more rigid, what would be possible if you brought in more flexibility?

Takeaway:

Being flexible is more advantageous than rigidity and chaos. Flexibility in your time management involves being willing to change your management tactics with an emphasis on having things work and produce outcomes (i.e. what gets accomplished) rather than an attachment to how it gets done.

NOTES:

URGENCY VS. EMERGENCY

From my own observations, most people get stressed out unnecessarily.

The amount of stress they go through does not seem to be worth it.

Yet many people continue to stress themselves out unnecessarily. It follows the definition of insanity: doing the same thing over and over again, but getting the same outcomes or less: they think that if they stress themselves out over and over again, something will change and they will get more or better outcomes.

This rarely works. There are many reasons for this insanity: but I will cover one reason in this section:

Reason: Most people don't have the distinction between emergency and urgency.

- **In emergency:** you don't have too much time to consider strategies or options. E.g. when you are having a heart attack, you have no time to think about all the options to resolve it and you need to act and call 911. There are costly and risky consequences if you don't act fast. It may be appropriate to choose quickly and to elevate your stress levels so that you can react quick and fast.

- **In urgency:** you have time to consider strategies and options. E.g. you have to generate income for the next month's rent payment. While there are costly and risky consequences potentially, you have more time to consider strategies and options. It may not be appropriate to elevate stress levels to react quick and fast.

The trouble is that most people mistake urgent situations for emergency situations and elevate stress to unnecessary levels. They also add to the stress by thinking that they have to handle the situation today or right away.

Takeaway:

Emergency is when you have no or little time to consider or think through your response before danger or risk is abnormally high. Urgency is where you have more time to consider or think and decide on the best course of action. Urgency is a good flow state to get into. Emergency is not necessarily a good flow state to be in (even if it feels like it may be with the adrenaline rush).

Get into Action:

Make a list of what you are worried about

For each item on your list, indicate how long you have before you get into emergency mode (you may have to guess this)

Based on your analysis above, which items are really urgent and which constitute emergencies?

Check your analysis with a trusted friend, coach or mentor to verify your thinking

NOTES:

Sunil Bhaskaran

Unnecessary Stress

I am going to suggest something that may sound quite revolutionary but is really quite sensible.

Consider stress to be an expense. If you are going to be stressed out and you choose to be stressed out or to remain stressed out, then make sure that whatever you are trying to achieve is worth being stressed out.

If it is not worth being stressed out, then start taking actions to reduce your stress immediately!

This includes the actions and practices that I recommend in this book as well as getting advice from your doctor and other health professionals.

The typical rewards for stress could be

- Growth or learning for you

- Profit or money coming back to you

- Long term satisfaction

Stress can cost you your life, health, relationships and your ability to lead, sell and make money – I would suggest strongly that you start increasing your awareness of stress and if it is really worth stressing out whenever you are stressed out.

Takeaway:

If you are stressed out, make sure that it is really worthwhile being stressed out

Questions to Ponder

Where are you experiencing unnecessary stress?

Where do you think you need to be stressed slightly to increase your challenge level so that you get out of boredom or stagnation?

What are the differences between unnecessary stress and stress that is necessary / required for growth to occur?

NOTES:

Long Term Suffering or Long term Joy ?

There is always a fork in the road so to speak for everyone: a decision in every moment. You are either going to live a life based in long term suffering or long term joy.

Most people tend to tolerate long term suffering (e.g. consistently complaining about something for days, months, years or decades.. or their entire life) in order to have short spurts of joy (e.g. feeling the short spurt of joy of a distraction e.g. Facebook, putting someone down in a conversation, or gossiping or drinking alcohol or overeating or having sex or having coffee or watching a movie etc.). This is not a wrong way to live: it is just possibly very ineffective.

People who tend to be successful in all areas of life also tend to be the opposite of the people I just described. They tend to be people who are willing to 'suffer' or stress for short periods of time (foregoing pleasure in the short term or going through some stress and hardship in the short term) in order to have longer term joy or happiness or satisfaction.

Why is this relevant to you in this training?

Very often in the pursuit of more time, more money and less stress, most people are very unwilling to give up bad habits that tend to have them tolerate suffering for a long time and have short spurts of joy from time to time in some attempt to make up for their chronic dissatisfaction.

If you fall into this category, you may want to consider strongly the costs of living your life in long term suffering/short spurts of joy.

Takeaway:

You can always choose between two worlds

- Long Term Stress associated with Short Spurts of Joy (escape)

- Short Term Stress associated with Long Term Joy (generative and outcome based)

Which do you prefer?

Get into Action:

Identify at least 10 areas in your life where you are tolerating long term suffering with short spurts of joy

For each of these areas, identify what it costs you and others around you when you engage in long term suffering

For each of these areas, identify what reasons or benefits you have to continue engaging in long term suffering

Sunil Bhaskaran

For each of these areas, ask yourself "Is it worth continuing to be in Long Term Suffering?"

NOTES:

ONE OF THE BEST WAYS TO GET AHEAD AND OUT OF THE RUT/PLATEAU YOU MAY BE IN: PLANNING

Most people have a short term view of their life: They plan mostly for the day or the next few hours and rarely over the next week and even more rarely over the month or the year.

There is a resistance to planning for most people for the following reasons they give:

- I can't really predict how things are going to go anyway: so what is the point of planning?

- My planning in the past has been a waste of time: it never worked out well for me

- I'm just not very good at planning: Help!

- By the time I plan it out, I can actually just get into action and make it happen anyway

Of course there could be other reasons as well but these are the ones that I typically hear.

There is a strong correlation between high stress levels and the comments above based on my own experience in coaching people.

Planning (long term) tends to alleviate stress and increase clarity because it gives you a long view of your time – which gives you the ability to 'spread' activities out over a longer time – you don't have to do everything today, this week or even this year.

Takeaway:

Planning reduces stress by giving you a long term view

Get into Action:

Schedule a time daily to plan your next day (Monday through Thursday at least – preferably at the end of your work time)

Make sure that you have enough time for all that you plan to do

Is the plan and schedule realistic? If not, make it more conservative and less ambitious.

Make sure that you have enough time to eat and nurture yourself.

NOTES:

CRITICAL FACTOR FOR PERFORMANCE IS INTEGRITY

Integrity has many definitions. However there is one definition that has worked very well for me and my successful clients. It is a definition that is given in different forms in different dictionaries.

The definition: The state of being whole and complete with nothing missing or left out OR the state of unity.

The word integrity itself comes from the Latin word for a finger representing the number one – indicating unity or the state of nothing missing – whole and complete.

Why is this definition critical to performance, peace of mind and more time, more money and less stress?

Let's take a deeper look via an example: Consider a bicycle wheel with spokes. If one spoke was missing, you would say that that wheel is out of integrity: not whole and complete: it has something missing.

Not a problem for the bike rider if she is going at slow speeds but to increase her speed and performance, she will have to put in what is missing: the spoke. The moment she puts in that spoke, the capacity for higher performance goes up.

Let's take an even deeper look.

When you have nothing missing in your life: what do you have to worry about in that moment?

Most people say "Nothing".

(Now it is accurate to say that your brain given that you are human will always try to find something new to worry about in the next moment: But for the moment that you have nothing missing in your life: you have nothing to worry about).

What does it mean to have nothing missing in your life?

Does that mean you have fixed or resolved everything?

Isn't that unrealistic?

You don't have to fix everything in your life in order to have things be whole and complete.

This is where Accountability comes in: if you account for everything that is missing in your life (e.g. you know you have a tax bill due and you have accounted for it by having a payment plan with due dates and amounts), then you have literally nothing missing really and... nothing to worry about.

So you could say that Accountability is one expression (and a darned important and good expression) of integrity.

This is a much more freed up and flexible definition of Accountability: To account for your promised outcomes (implied or explicit promised outcomes) leads to more freedom.

Get into Action: Questions to Ponder

List out the areas where you feel something is missing e.g. an unresolved communication e.g. an unresolved promised outcome made by you to yourself e.g. an unresolved promised outcome from you to others e.g. an unresolved promised outcome made by someone else to you e.g. an unexpressed communication etc.

What would it be like if you could complete each and every one of these?

What would be different in your life? In your business? In your relationships?

For each item, choose if you are going to resolve these now or in the future.

Accept the possible consequences for whatever your response is to the last question i.e. accept the consequences for resolving or not resolving the item.

For those items that you choose to be in action, schedule these actions into your calendar

Takeaway:

Accounting for your promised outcomes (implied or explicit) results in freedom and peace of mind and… performance increases. Accountability is an expression of integrity. Take note of any promised outcomes unaccounted for. How can you account for each promised outcome? Get into action to account for each promised outcome.

NOTES:

DECISION AND OUTCOME CREATION 101

Your ability to make decisions and create clear outcomes will affect the level of flow, productivity and peace of mind in your life and in your business.

DECISION AND OUTCOME CREATION: IN YOUR BRAIN: EMOTIONS AND RATIONAL

When it comes to making a decision or creating clear outcomes, your brain acts like a 'parliament of voices'[xxv].

The two primary voices are:

- Emotional

- Rational/Moral

These two voices are actually physically represented in the brain matter by two separate brain circuits.

The brain resolves decision and outcome creation using these two brain circuits.

You may be able to see why we get stuck in our decision making now. If your emotions say one thing and your rational or moral part say something else, you have a conflict and you feel stuck in making decisions.

DECISION AND OUTCOME CREATION: STOPS

I will go over some of the stops or blocks in making clear decisions and clear outcomes. The intention is that with that understanding, you can in a practical sense be more likely to make clearer outcomes and clearer decisions.

Stop 1: Conflict

Most people do not attain outcomes primarily because they have conflicting outcomes or beliefs: they have outcomes or beliefs (which express outcomes in some form) that are in conflict with each other e.g. John has an outcome of spending at least 40 hours a week for 40 weeks in a year with his family and also has an outcome of increasing his income by 20 percent for this year compared to last year – John feels conflicted because he thinks that in order to make more money this year, he has to actually spend less time with his family and more time on his business.

These conflicts are sometimes subconscious - resolving the conflicts results in clarity and movement forward.

Exercise:
List out your outcomes for the year
Identify which outcomes are not progressing fast enough for you

Do your best to identify any conflicts if any between your outcomes

Stop 2: Out of Integrity

The mind tends to like being in integrity although it may resist the actions to get there. When something is not complete, the mind tends to not be at rest and tends to be distracted. This is based more on my own observations being a coach.

When things get back into integrity, there is less distraction and with the released energy (due partly from hormones like dopamine), you are more likely to make clearer minded decisions.

Exercise:

Notice times in the past where you resisted getting something complete (e.g. calling someone back, e.g. getting your taxes done e.g. repaying someone back fully, etc.).

For each of these times, what was it like for you (what was the experience like) when you actually, finally got the issue or desired outcome complete?

Section Two: A New Context for You – Concerning Your Time, Money & Stress Reduction

Sunil Bhaskaran

THE INTENTION OF THIS SECTION

The intention of this section is to help you reframe time management into a different and more useful context - a context that will empower you, help you make more money in less time and create more freedom for you.

Most people think about time management as managing their time – they think that just by managing their time blocks or getting better at managing their time, they will get better at producing outcomes or that by just merely thinking about how to get more done, they will improve productivity or quality of life.

In fact, in most cases that I have seen of people attempting to better manage their time, they fail to manage both time and their outcomes as well as their ability to create a lifestyle that works for them.

Perhaps it is of little interest to manage time – after all who cares so much about managing time or time blocks?

I am more interested in managing my promised outcomes. Notice how that feels or resonates with your mind and feelings as you read this statement:

"Maybe it is more useful to manage your promised outcomes than in managing your time"

Get into Action:

"Maybe it is more useful to manage your promised outcomes than in managing your time"

When you say this to yourself, notice how you feel and how this statement resonates (or does not resonate) with you. Write down any insights, thoughts or feelings about this point.

What would be different for you and your business/career if you kept a higher number of promised outcomes (e.g. to yourself, to your business, to your career, to your health, to your family) than you do now?

NOTES:

50

BECOMING A MASTER PLANNER AND 'PRIORITIZER'

As an entrepreneur (or as a professional), your job is to make sure that your service or product is delivered on time and efficiently and effectively to your clients (or your employer/manager/team/company). This requires you to become a Master Planner.

Becoming a master planner is a step up from being a time manager.

As a maturing entrepreneur, professional or lay person, it is imperative to learn how to plan and prioritize. Planning and prioritizing are the best high profit activities that you can perform – and it can also take up the most energy.

There are two quick practices to do when you start your day (or week, or month or year).

Visualize what your outcomes will look like (e.g. a completed book with all the chapters set out correctly e.g. 100 new clients meeting you at your company end of the year party e.g. a completed 1st section of the 1st chapter of your book for the end of the day). Visual functions in the brain are very well developed: there are about 30 different parts of your brain that process visual information from the eye to enable you to 'see'. This processing is mostly in the unconscious parts of the brain but is very efficient and effective and takes far less energy to do. This is why some people find it easier to 'see' an answer rather than read about it. I advocate visualizing the outcomes first for the day, week, month or year and then writing it down.

Start the day out with prioritizing and planning your main outcomes rather than spending precious brain energy on distractions (e.g. emails that are not that important, Facebook postings that are not critical, etc.) If your work depends on emails, then do a quick glance over your emails to handle only highly urgent or emergency emails; if there are no urgent or emergency emails, then move on to the planning or prioritizing as soon as possible.

If you train yourself like this every day, you will start seeing the benefits of planning and prioritizing:

We have seen our clients (who consistently plan) learn to enjoy planning. Planning is not necessarily a pleasure, but it can be enjoyed. (See the distinction between pleasure and enjoyment at the beginning of this book).

Your stress starts going down as you create more clarity in what your steps are in the future.

Planning (especially planning for the long term) tends to enable you to spread your outcomes and projects out over a longer period, leading to more free time for you to innovate and create more ideas and better ways to execute on the ideas you already are working on.

Sunil Bhaskaran

Planning long term also tends to reduce risks – being able to foresee potential breakdowns, obstacles and problems and be able to handle them ahead of time.

Get into Action

Visualize your top four to seven outcomes for the month: what do they look like to you when accomplished?

Of these four to seven, which are the highest priority outcomes? List out the priorities from highest to lowest priority.

Of these, which are the absolute top two that you need to focus on?

Why?

What would become possible in your future, if you became a master planner and master 'prioritizer'?

NOTES:

OUTCOME ORIENTATION: QUEEN/KING BEE VS. WORKER BEE

I would much rather help you become Queen Bees or King Bees than Worker Bees.

Queen Bee or King Bee[xxvi] is a metaphor for someone who is out to produce outcomes and keep their promised outcomes. 'Worker Bee' is a metaphor for someone who is out to do ever increasing amounts of work.

To become efficient and balanced in your use of time, you want to consider shifting your mindset to an outcome orientation (Queen or King Bee) vs. a task or work orientation (Worker Bee)

A Queen/King Bee generates and focuses his/her management and attention on outcomes.

A worker bee tends to generate activity, but does not necessarily have the viewpoint or inclination to manage overall outcomes and to see if his/her actions really add up to the company or organizational long term vision and outcomes.

Get into Action:

Notice where you are a Queen Bee/King Bee in life and where you are a Worker Bee.

What are the costs and benefits of being a Worker Bee?

What are the costs and benefits of being a Queen or King Bee?

NOTES:

LEVERAGE AND YOUR BEST AND HIGHEST USE

Also as a Queen Bee/King Bee, you are committed to expending energy only in the direction of what is your best and highest use – where you can best leverage your highest skills into the working of your enterprise.

This implies that you do some forethought and planning on a consistent basis.

This forethought and planning includes looking at the options for activities or outcomes and determining what would be the best combination of activities and outcomes that will optimize the profit and satisfaction for you and for your business/career/company/team.

When you manage your finances, you do the same process as in the previous paragraph on selecting the best portfolio of your assets (e.g. real estate, gold, stocks and bonds, IRAs, 401ks, retirement savings, etc.)

The best combination of your outcomes and activities will give you the best return on investment (the outcomes that you generate e.g. your profit or what you get paid vs. your time, energy and money put in to these outcomes) with the least amount of risk.

Questions to Ponder

What would the benefit be to you in your business, life and career to start assessing how to get the best combination of outcomes and activities to increase/ optimize your return on investment with the least risk?

What do you see could be different for you if you adopted such an approach to your life, business or career?

MOVING FROM TIME MANAGEMENT TO OUTCOME MANAGEMENT

Being outcome focused, shifts your thinking away from managing time or time blocks towards what that time usage can produce in terms of outcomes. If you think like this, you will be looking at producing more outcomes in less time and perhaps with much less stress.

Many clients, when they first come to me, keep thinking in terms of actions or activity.

Nothing wrong with that way of thinking – it certainly beats not doing anything at all.

However, task or action based thinking does not necessarily produce outcomes nor does it give you immediate access to thinking about how to leverage and manage your resources (e.g. time, energy and money) to produce the most outcomes.

e.g.

Sales person A measures their activity: so she measures the number of sales calls being done daily, weekly, monthly and yearly.

Sales person B measures their outcomes: so she measures the number of sales appointments, referrals and actual sales produced daily, weekly, monthly and yearly.

Person A will probably tend towards making the calls and then stopping there. If she is lucky or a good sales person, she may be able to make a decent living off her already acquired skills. If she is not measuring or managing outcomes (e.g. referrals, sales, appointments) she will be less likely to produce these outcomes.

Person B has the following advantages over Person A

- They have the focus and attention on what really matters: actual outcomes leading to productivity, satisfaction and less stress over time. Having clarity can actually reduce stress in the long run – stress can result out of a feeling of lacking in clarity and control over a situation.

- They can see which of their tasks or actions are ineffective: i.e. these tasks or activities do not add up to the outcomes they want or are inefficient (i.e. they require a lot of effort to produce the same outcome).

Questions to Ponder
Which would you prefer to be : Person A or B?
Why?
What are the benefits and disadvantages of Person B?
What are the benefits and disadvantages of Person A?

Sunil Bhaskaran

MOVING FROM TIME MANAGEMENT TO PROMISED OUTCOME MANAGEMENT – BUILDING YOUR RELIABILITY

Keeping promised outcomes increases your reliability – both to yourself as well as to other people including your team, clients, family, friends and other members of your communities. This in turn builds your leadership abilities and your organization's strength/foundation.

Reliability = the percentage of times that you keep a promised outcome in a domain

e.g. The author's reliability in performing heart surgery on another human being and have that human being's heart operating perfectly again is very low (To this date, the author has not performed a single heart operation successfully and neither does he intend to in the short term). However, the author's ability to coach someone to success is quite high based on the historical evidence: number of promised outcomes kept to clients vs. promised outcomes made in totality.

Get into Action:

Identify the top 6 domains in your life e.g. work, health, relationships, etc. that you value. For each, rate your reliability to produce outcomes or to keep your promised outcomes.

NOTES:

REVIEW – DEFINITION OF AN OUTCOME

An outcome must have all of the following

- A deadline date and time e.g. by end of Dec 31st 2012 e.g. by the end of today 11:59 pm

- A number and/or observable event or a defined experience e.g. I will have our checking account have at least $250,000 (number) by end of Dec 21st 2012   e.g. I will have the report on your desk (observable event) by 12 noon this Friday e.g. I will feel satisfied

- Something that you are willing to put at stake to have this promised outcome happen e.g. I am willing to devote 20 hours a week to make this promised outcome happen e.g. I am willing to stake my complete reputation to make this promised outcome happen. The degree to which you put something at stake expresses to yourself and others the degree of commitment to this outcome. After all, what is the point of creating an outcome if you have very little at stake in getting it accomplished? You may be spending a lot of your resources of time, energy, money and team time to get an outcome accomplished. Wouldn't it make sense for you to make sure that there is sufficient at stake for yourself to get this outcome done?

Examples of outcomes are your promised outcomes and goals. An outcome could have a deadline date of a few minutes through several years.

Questions to Ponder / Get into Action

Review the outcomes (e.g. goals and promised outcomes) that you have now
Is each outcome defined well enough using the criteria above?
If not, how will you make it clearer for yourself?
How will your life and business/career be different if you adopt this way of clarifying outcomes i.e. goals, promised outcome?

Sunil Bhaskaran

Practices vs. Outcomes

I have many new clients who come up with outcomes that are not really outcomes but are actually practices.

Example:
"Working out every week: three times a week" is not an outcome – it is a practice – it has no deadline date and is repetitive.

"I will work out a total 20 hours and be able to lift at least 100 lbs in my bench press exercise by the end of this month" is an outcome.

It is okay to have practices, but please be clear about the distinction between practices and outcomes. A practice is an activity that is done at some frequency – it is not an outcome. A practice can help fulfill on an outcome (e.g. goal or promised outcome): but a practice is not an outcome.

An example of how you can use practices to fulfill on an outcome:

To help fulfill on the outcome "I will work out a total 20 hours and be able to lift at least 100 lbs in my bench press exercise by the end of this month", I will practice bench press exercises at least 4 times a week with a fitness trainer for the rest of the month.

The best way to manage practices is to schedule them into your calendar, whilst an outcome is something that is more complex than a practice and will at times require more than a calendar to manage to success.

Why is this distinction useful?

When people treat something which is a practice as an outcome, they set themselves up to lose: if they miss one practice event (e.g. one workout day), they have failed the entire outcome. When you create a practice that is done frequently you are liable to miss one or two practice days; why set yourself up to lose unnecessarily?

Questions to ponder / Get into action

Review the outcomes that you have now

Identify any practices and start treating these as practices and not outcomes

WINNABLE OUTCOMES

My invitation to you is to make outcomes (e.g. goals, promised outcomes) that set you up to win:

Have the outcomes be reachable outcomes: make sure that you have the necessary resources or the desire to get the necessary resources to make the outcome happen.

Set up the outcomes well: Numbers and/or observable events made very clear. Outcomes should be set up as numbers (e.g. I will make at least $250 today) or observable events (e.g. I will have the report on your desk by 5 pm today)

Start with simple outcomes: Don't try to get the perfect outcomes – you will get the perfect outcome as you fine tune and revisit your plan daily. Simply start. Start first. Start now – start with a guess, then refine your outcome as you get feedback on your performance.

All outcomes are guesses when you first start out. A good outcome is one which you can fine-tune as you go along based on what the existing conditions are and what makes sense.

Don't set up outcomes that say you will attain something "every month" or "every week" i.e. avoid outcomes like these e.g. "I will workout every week by the end of December 2012" – if you set up this way, you are setting up for failure – e.g. if you miss just one week, you would have failed!

Set up outcomes that set you up to win – e.g. I will work out at least 20 days of the next 50 days – this way, if you miss one day, you can still catch up to win.

Start with low win-able outcomes and with the intention of consistently stretching yourself to get better over time.

Questions to ponder

What would your life, business or career look like if you adopted the above policies in creating winnable outcomes?

If you have a team - what would be possible for your team based on the distinctions presented above?

NOTES:

Sunil Bhaskaran

How to Decide Which Outcomes to Spend time On - High Profit and Satisfaction Centers

Your time is arguably your best and maybe only true resource. All you have towards the end of your life, is the notion of having spent your time well.. or perhaps not that well. Maybe time is your only true resource?

I like to look at time as an asset – very much like a financial asset (e.g. an investment, a business , real estate, etc.). It is a limited resource or asset. Like all limited assets, you want to manage in the following manner:

- Reduce the risk associated with using that asset

- Increase what you can get out of using that asset (Return)

- Reduce what you expend into that asset or make sure that what you expend (or invest) gives you a good enough return or profit that justifies both the risk and the expense as much as possible.

If you wish to be an expert in investing, you would consider the 3 points above very strongly.

I invite you to do the same consideration with how you spend your time. I invite you to use the three points in helping you decide what outcomes you wish to spend time on and how much time to spend on such an outcome.

When you select which outcomes to focus on, you will want to consider the following:

- Reduce Risks: Reduce as much as possible, the risk associated with using an amount of your time, money and other resources for an outcome

- Increase Returns: Increase as much as possible what you can get out of using that amount of time on an outcome

- Reduce the Investment: Reduce as much as possible the time that you spend on an outcome or make sure that what you expend gives you a good enough return or profit that justifies both the risk and the expense as much as possible

You can use the analysis above to help you decide where to spend time: i.e. on which outcomes or which combination of outcomes.

Please bear in mind that this analysis still requires some subjective input: this process will not give you a magically correct answer to what and where to spend your time on – but the process is still useful to have as a means of thinking through your decision making process of deciding where to spend your time on i.e. on which outcomes in your business or life.

Example:

You have to choose between either Outcome A or Outcome B: How could I do this?

Here are the guesses for risk, return and investment for each Outcome

Outcome A: Website Bio Page

Risk: Low Risk – very little chance of legal threats and other issues

Potential Return in One Year: 2 more speaking engagements worth potentially about $10,000 (the improved biography on the website can attract more and potentially better speaking engagements)

Investment: 2 hours of my time (at $400/hr => $800) + web designer ($200) = about $1,000 total

Return on Investment = Potential Return/Investment = $10,000/$1,000 = 10 x return

Outcome B: Hire New Full time Admin

Risk: High - He/She may not work out, He/she may upset my clients and cause a loss of clientele not to mention ruin my reputation

Potential Return in One Year: Savings in my time could be in the order of 3 hours a week -> 150 hours a year -> $60,000 per year (at $400 per hour – 400 * 150 =60,000)

Investment: $1,000 per month -> $12,000 per year

Return on Investment = $60,000/$12,000 = 5 x return

There is no hard and fast rule about which is the better choice: but I want you to get the thinking here rather than a quick answer.

Takeaway:

Treat your time like a valuable financial asset – start assessing the risk, return and investment for your time use and for the outcomes that you pick.

Get into Action:

Questions for discussion or for thought:

If you could only do either Outcome A or Outcome B, which outcome would you choose to do and why? What are the other variables that you have to consider?

If you could do both, what could you do to make both work and reduce risks and increase the return? What are the other variables that you have to consider?

What would be different for your life, career or business if you adopted this kind of analysis for what you chose to focus your energies on?

NOTES:

IS WHAT YOU ARE DOING BUILDING UP TO SOMETHING WORTHWHILE?

One of the primary reasons for stress is that people don't have the experience of clarity or control over their day to day outcomes – specifically they don't know or seemingly cannot see if what they are doing today will add up to something substantial in the next year or so.

Research has revealed that people are more inclined to meet their outcomes if their outcomes are longer term oriented. (e.g. they are more likely to hit monthly/yearly outcomes than weekly outcomes)[xxvii]

However, in my experience coaching people, I have found that people also need to see whether their daily outcomes are adding up to their monthly and yearly outcomes.

This reduces stress while giving an experience of being more in control.

I recommend creating and managing both your short term (daily/weekly) and longer term outcomes (monthly or yearly or longer).[xxviii]

Takeaway:

Manage daily, monthly and yearly outcomes. Schedule a time every week at least to review these outcomes to see if you are on track or off track.

Questions to Ponder / Get into Action

Are you currently planning your days and weeks in advance?

Are you currently planning your months ahead and the next year in advance?

How often do you refine your plan?

What are the benefits of planning?

What are the costs of planning?

How can you mitigate the costs of planning for yourself so you can reap the benefits of planning?

NOTES:

GETTING MORE DONE WITH LESS: REALISTIC PLANNING

Let dopamine work for you - not against you

Research[xxix] has revealed that when you fail to meet expectations, your dopamine levels go down.

The opposite is true when your expectations are met – when your expectations are met or exceeded, your dopamine levels go up. Dopamine is a naturally occurring chemical in your brain that keeps you motivated and confident.

So when you fail to meet expectations, your level of confidence and motivation goes down, leading to a downward spiral in energy overall.

When you meet or exceed your expectations, your level of confidence and motivation goes up, leading to an upward spiral.

Questions to Ponder / Get into Action

Are you currently managing your expectations well e.g. are your expectations on a daily, weekly, monthly and yearly basis realistic or unrealistic?

How would you know the answer to the question posed in above? (HINT: Look at your outcomes: are they meeting what you expect or plan?)

How would managing your expectations realistically affect your stress levels?

How would managing your expectations realistically affect your profit levels or the income you make or your finances?

Takeaway:

If you manage your expectations well, you can manage your confidence and motivation levels. Plan realistically for your expectations (and then gradually stretch yourself daily to increase your skill and challenge level) and you will have more good/productive/motivated days.

NOTES:

Sunil Bhaskaran

More than four... almost never happens

Many years ago, I did a little research on my client's productivity levels. What I found was when people come to me with a list of more than 4 project items, they typically got (on an average) zero items done. Interesting things happened when they reduced the number of items: when they picked only four or less items to focus on for that day, they would get between 50 to 75 percent[xxx] done by about 2 pm in the afternoon (assuming they started at 9 am latest).[xxxi]

What I have also seen is that with some practice, people can increase the number from four upwards. This involves the same principle as in body building or weight training. When you first start, you start with what your body or brain can handle (i.e. the biological or current mental limits). Then you gradually increase the weights and maybe even very occasionally do a greater leap in weights to keep growing and improving your skill. It is this combination of increasing skill and challenge that creates the experience of flow and energy.[xxxii]

Takeaway:

Identify and prioritize the top four outcomes that you intend to fulfill on for the week and review this daily

NOTES:

THE PATH TO FREEDOM AND FOCUS : RULE OF FOUR

Rule of Four is a practice that we do with people in our coaching programs.

The idea behind the Rule of Four is to limit your highest priority outcomes for the day, week, month or year to four.

These are four that you are primarily going to focus on for the day, week, month of year. You may have more than four that you may find important: but I want to train you to focus more energy on the highest priority items. The mantra could be said in this way: "Do fewer things really well rather than many things badly or not as well".

In my coaching programs, I found that people get optimum outcomes by focusing on four or less outcomes at a time. Based in brain science, we know that the prefrontal cortex (part of the brain responsible for most day to day work including understanding, memory, managing impulses, deciding, task switching, etc.) does not operate well when inundated with too many projects or tasks – it is inefficient in memory space (quite like a computer with low memory) and inefficient in how it expends and uses energy.

Therefore the Rule of Four helps manage inside of this biological limitation: the rule of four keeps it real and keeps you effective!

You can train yourself to do a little more than four – this takes practice and can be done over time.

Takeaway:

Rule of Four implies doing four or less outcomes per day, week, month and year.

NOTES:

Sunil Bhaskaran

CREATING MORE BLANK SPACE ON YOUR SCHEDULE

When I became an entrepreneur, one of the things that I determined to do was to create as much free space on my schedule as possible. I enjoyed working and still do enjoy working. Sometimes I choose to work long hours – these long hours are by choice. That is the main point that I wish to make – that you can choose to work long hours, short hours or no hours.. but that is by your choice... not by compulsion.

An entrepreneur (if you are a working professional, I still invite you to think as an entrepreneur within your company), deserves to have as much free time as possible for taking the risks of starting and running an enterprise.

But talk is cheap: you need measures to express this freedom and free time. I have found a good measure and dashboard for tracking this freedom of time via measuring blank space on your calendar. This blank space expresses time that you have – this time that has no obligation associated with it – you are free to choose what you focus on during these blank times.

Hence the more blank times you have, the more freedom you have i.e. the more freedom of choice that you have.

Now I also understand that this may be difficult to arrive at. Some of you have financial constraints – I am not pretending that you don't and I don't intend on giving you some Pollyanna like advice.

The question perhaps to ask is "How can I make more free time happen?"

The answer is to accomplish this intentionally in small steps and over time:

- Start with low expectations: every week try to create a little more free time

- Ascertain how much free time you have now e.g. you may only have 7 hours of free time realistically a week now.

- For the first week or two, start small e.g. if you currently only have 7 hours of free time a week, build it up to 7 hours and 15 minutes for a few weeks.

- Then for the third and fourth week, bump it up a little bit e.g. to 7 hours and 45 minutes.

- Build up slowly till you have more free time without compromising your efficiency

Get into Action

- Start with low expectations: every week try to create a little more free time

- Ascertain how much free time you have now e.g. you may only have 7 hours of free time realistically a week now.

- For the first week or two, start small e.g. if you currently only have 7 hours of free time a week, build it up to 7 hours and 15 minutes for a few weeks.

- Then for the third and fourth week, bump it up a little bit to 7 hours and 45 minutes.

- Build up slowly till you have more free time without compromising your efficiency

IF YOU ARE WORKING FOR SOMEONE ELSE OR A COMPANY,

- Do the same steps above

- Take steps to communicate with your boss regarding your plans to increase your free time or time with your family

- Create reasonable targets for free time with your boss for the next few months and indicate or offer what you may be willing to do in exchange in terms of improved performance or coming in earlier, promised outcomes to better work and keep your schedule, etc.

- I understand that you may be dealing with certain politics and policies within the company that make this difficult: but the first step is always critical – i.e. taking steps to communicate and then negotiate for your needs

NOTES:

SAFE AND SANE OUTCOME MANAGEMENT STRATEGIES

The mechanics of time management are important, but not as important as thinking about outcomes or promised outcomes first. If you figure out clearly what your promised outcomes are, then the mechanics of time management become more straightforward and dare I say it, actually easier and more fun to do.

Get into Action:

There are four primary practices to start employing with regards to your outcome management:

- Be sure to use one and only one calendar to capture any promised outcomes that you make to others or to yourself. If you use one calendar for your personal life and one for your work life, you may be risking some degree of double booking both calendars – but if you find this separation of two calendars difficult, continue with two, but do make sure that the calendars are clearly delineated by the range of hours e.g. work calendar only from 8 am to 6 pm and personal calendar only from 6 pm to 8 am the next day.

- Then actually use your calendar to capture all promised outcomes that you make to others and to yourself – no exceptions. Stop relying on your biological memory to store your promised outcomes and appointments. Your biological memory is highly unreliable.[xxxiii]

- Start the practice of spreading your time blocks on your calendar out over a longer time frame. What most people do is to squeeze a lot into one week or one day or one month – the schedule or calendar looks packed and overwhelming just to look at. Spread out your time blocks. This creates more blank space on your calendar. This may be difficult for some of you to do: people think that they have to get everything done fast. But the reality is that people almost never get all or even a reasonable percentage of what they said they will accomplish, accomplished in the time that they indicate. What is the point of continuing to live inside of this lack of reality? The second counter argument I get is that they want to stretch or challenge themselves every week and if they don't put in more outcomes than they can get done, they will get none done at all. I say do what works: but if it is not working for you, and the extra challenge is not stretching you but causing you more stress than putting money, satisfaction and outcomes back in your pocket, it may be time to think of a more sane and rational approach to creating breakthroughs.

- Be sure to have blank space (at least 15 minutes) in between each block: this will help you to spread out the time blocks so that you are not inundated with work and get overwhelmed. This may seem nitpicky, but you do want to follow this strategy very rigorously – the accounting for your time is very important to do. Realistically you will need this 15 minute of buffer time; nobody is able to end an appointment on time all the time and then be able to immediately switch gears mentally or physically to be ready for their next appointment right away – some transition or blank time is necessary to be able to seamlessly move from one appointment or time block of project work to another.

- Make sure that you schedule a time at the end of your day or the start of your day to clean up your calendar so that it reflects these rules above for your future day or week.

- As you get more sophisticated, there are more practices to learn to keep your time management safe and sane: but for now, these practices are a very good start.

Get into Action

What do you think your life will be like if you had safe and sane time management practices?

What would happen if you did not make changes to how you manage your time more efficiently and more effectively?

NOTES:

Sunil Bhaskaran

START WITH THE BIGGER PICTURE: START WITH THE 30,000 FOOT VIEW

Most people get very much stuck in their work because they are trying to make very low level decisions without looking at or remembering the bigger picture.

The bigger picture answers the following questions:

- What are your primary medium term to longer term objectives or outcomes?

- Why are you in business: what is the vision or mission of your business?

Re-starting with the bigger picture in mind when you get stuck will help you clarify your decisions pertaining to what to focus on for the short term (e.g. for the day or the week).

Get into Action:

Do you have a mission statement that inspires you (personally and for your company)?

What about the mission statement inspires you?

If you have no mission statement, start crafting one:

- Come up with a list of 10-20 words or phrases that inspire you (e.g. Making a Difference, Integrity, Bringing the Best Out of My Team, etc.)

- Fine tune this down to your best inspiring 5 words or phrases

- Try your best to combine these 5 words or phrases into a working mission statement

- Be flexible: if you feel one of the words or phrases you threw out works better with one already chosen, go ahead and use that combination and see if it lands for you.

- Nobody can tell you that your mission is wrong.

- Nobody can tell you if it is right either.

- You will know (especially over time) if the mission inspires action and outcomes or not.

- Be prepared to fine tune the mission statement over time

Are your longer term outcomes congruent with your mission statement?
If not, what needs to change: the mission and/or the outcomes?

Questions to ponder:

What would be different for you and your company if you started having your mission be rigorously congruent with your actions and long term outcomes?

NOTES:

How to Make Your Large Outcomes Easy and Do-able

When the brain first encounters a large complicated outcome, it will probably do an avoidance reaction. A part of the brain responsible for emotional reactions and fear may kick in (it typically does!).

To be effective then, it may behoove you to break down or chunk down your outcomes into smaller components.

Start tracking your promised outcomes for each day. If you are missing certain outcomes every day or often, the suggestion I have for you is to either

- Delay doing this outcome for a while OR

- Do a smaller chunk of this outcome in that day

In the next section, we will go over how you can start chunking down your outcomes.

NOTES:

How to Chunk Down

Steps involved

There are two methods to use: Chronological Chunk Down OR Functional Chunk Down

You could do a combination of these two methods to chunk down your outcomes.

Chronological Chunk Down

Essentially in this process, you break the outcome down into a sequence of milestones/outcomes

Start by sequencing these milestones or outcomes sequentially i.e. one after the other i.e. the next step cannot be done until the one before is accomplished.

Once you have these sequenced, then you can work on looking to see which outcomes can be handled in parallel (i.e. at the same time)

Parallel outcomes can be delegated to other people so that you don't have to end up doing it all (this is a very powerful hint!)

These milestones are steps along the way to fulfill on the ultimate outcome

Don't get too detailed to start with. You can improve on the details and refine milestones as you act on the plan.

The fundamental questions to ask as you write an outcome down

- What needs to happen first?

- What needs to happen before that?

- What needs to happen after that?

E.g. Milestones for the Outcome to 'Clear Garage within the next 30 days'

- Schedule a weekend to get this done

- Hire 2 college students to help

- Buy boxes

- Hire a truck

- Reconfirm College students four days before

- Create sequence of segments of the garage to work on: A plan to execute on for the day of the clearing

- Day Before: Pick up rental truck

- On day of: Greet students and meet to go over plan

- Have husband manage the plan and give me updates every 1 hour

- Pick up meals for everyone involved

- Pay college kids

- Next Day: Return Rental Truck

The next step would be to break these down into smaller outcomes or tasks if necessary

Then schedule times to do these tasks OR if you are going to devote a single block of time to the outcome (if it only requires a few hours for example), then use a temporary check-off list for the first time.

NOTES:

FUNCTIONAL CHUNK DOWN

In this method of chunking down outcomes, we look at the functions that need to be implemented to make the entire outcome work

An analogy would be a car building outcome: to build a car, you need a couple of main functions implemented e.g. Steering Function (to steer), Engine Function (to move it forward), Braking Function (to brake the car), Transmission Function (to transmit energy or power to the wheels), etc.

The fundamental question to ask in this process is

- What are the functions that I need to make this overall outcome work?

- Are these functions sufficient to make the outcome work to completion?

E.g. Clear Garage within the next 30 days

- Management Function: Manage the college kids and keep them on track (delegate to husband)

- Lifting and Clearing Function: Two college kids to lift and carry stuff and put into boxes

- Driving Function: Someone to drive the truck and take boxes to recycle depot or to places that will collect junk and dispose of it safely and in an environmentally friendly manner. I will do this.

- Food Order and Delivery Function: Get the food delivered and served to team. I will do this.

The next step would be to write up tasks or projects for each function and schedule times to execute.

NOTES:

Additional Note: MindMap

There are many Mind Mapping Software applications that are available to help you chunk down an outcome. For those interested in using MindMaps: Do an internet search for "Mind Mapping Software" or "Mind Map Software".

HEALTH AS A FOUNDATION

I am clear that without good health, no business owner can operate their business effectively. The costs of stress, insufficient exercise, lack of sleep, lack of water and lack of proper nutrition are just way too high.

The time, effort and money spent on improving health is not only preventative of risky sickness but also imperative in generating returns in your business i.e. the more you invest into health, the more likely are the returns to you (in terms of quality and quantity). Good health is good for your heart and for your brain. The better your brain performs, the more likely you are to be creative, sell more, make better decisions and relate and lead your team better.

Again, this may sound like another cliché – but remember – most clichés may sound boring, but they are unfortunately true and largely ignored. If you want to leap past your competition, you don't want to ignore this section.

There are four areas I want to cover here:[xxxiv]

- Exercise

- Nutrition

- Sleep

- Water

EXERCISE

Regular exercise is good for your brain. It promotes the growth of new brain cells (more brain cells implies more connections possible implies more intelligence implies more sales and better decisions). Exercise promotes circulation of the blood: Improved circulation also helps the elimination of toxins produced as a result of activity, as well as improved oxygen supply to the brain. The effects on reducing your stress are better understood today. Exercise also reduces chances of getting old age afflictions like Alzheimer's, memory loss etc. We, as human beings evolved to move. Our brains work better when we are in movement i.e. walking, running, exercising – not exercising results in dealing with diseases and afflictions like obesity that our ancestors did not have to deal with because.. they fundamentally got more exercise (probably) than most of us did – some studies point to the possibility that our ancestors walked/moved up to 20 miles or more per day! Not many of us do that much walking in a week!

Takeaway:

Bottom line: Exercise regularly!

Get into Action:

Get and schedule a medical checkup especially if you have not had one recently. Ask your doctor how often you can and should exercise

If you are already exercising, schedule times to exercise and gradually (very gradually) increase the frequency per week to at least 6 times a week of cardio (20 minutes each time).

If you have not exercised for a while, start slow: even walking for a few minutes every day is better than nothing – start with a ridiculously low number of minutes: 1 minute every 2 days – then build up.

NOTES:

NUTRITION

Your brain takes up 20 percent of your caloric input (your food that gets converted to energy). It behooves you to make sure that your brain is well fed especially if you are doing a lot of "brain work" daily. Your brain requires a consistent level of glucose in the blood: glucose gets converted into neurotransmitters in the brain: neurotransmitters help in moving electrical messages around in the brain and across the body: no or low glucose implies less neurotransmitters implies the brain starts slowing down and being unable to handle stress, inputs, decisions etc.

Takeaway:

Bottom line: Watch your nutrition closely!

Get into Action:

If you can afford it, hire a good nutritionist to advise you on what you need to eat to optimize your energy

Make sure that you spread out your eating over the day to keep your blood sugar (glucose) levels sufficient: not too high and not too low.

NOTES:

Sunil Bhaskaran

Sleep

Of all the most common complaints I receive, lack of sleep is one of the more common ones. The brain needs sleep for restoration, improving immunity, reducing stress, etc.

Get into Action:

Notice if you are a lark or owl:[xxxv] A lark is someone who tends to go to bed early and arise early in the morning. An owl is the opposite: sleep later and wake up later. There is nothing wrong with either way of sleeping. Note down which category you fall under: owl or lark. Also note when you fall asleep naturally and when you awake naturally. Then schedule your work and life around these hours as best as you can. Taking naps in the middle of the day is one of the best things that you can do to help restore your brain function: I do this myself – I take afternoon naps very frequently – the return on investment in napping is very high for me. I used to do this even when I worked in the corporate environment – I would take a nap in my car under the shade and come back much more productive than my co-workers who strove to force themselves through the day with coffee, tea, pep drinks – usually after a very heavy lunch.

Make sure that you spread out your eating over the day to keep your blood sugar (glucose) levels sufficient: not too high and not too low.

NOTES:

PURE WATER

The Recommended Dietary Allowance[xxxvi] for water for men is 3.7 liters or about 10 to 15 cups per day. This will seem like quite a lot of water for most of us – most of us don't even drink one half of this amount! But that is what is required for healthy functioning of your organs and your body including your brain.

I observed the importance of water in my own life: I tracked my water consumption for three months and observed very clearly that the days on which my water consumption dipped below 6 cups were the days that I performed worst (hardest to make decisions, productivity in terms of outcomes was low, I became snappy and irritable more) – not the most scientifically conducted experiment, but was nonetheless very convincing to me.

Takeaway:

Bottom line: Drink More Pure Water!

Get into Action:

Work out the minimum water you need per your body weight based on the Recommended Dietary Allowance (see End Notes in this book or do a search on the internet for the latest RDA on water consumption – they will typically tell you how much to expect to drink based on your weight or give you a calculator to help you figure this out)

Start slow: if you are only drinking 4 cups a day, start with 4 cups a day. Then in one week, build up slowly to 5 cups a day. Then keep building up every week until you hit your RDA.

NOTES:

Sunil Bhaskaran

REVIEW: THE #1 KEY TO PERFORMANCE = RELIABILITY

If you really think about it, the key to performance and increasing it is to become more reliable: i.e. More reliable in keeping your promised outcomes.

The more reliable you are in keeping your promised outcomes, the more reliable you will be considered by yourself and by others.

i.e. the more that you say X happens and X actually happens, the more reliable you are considered in the domain of whatever X lies.

e.g. if the domain is "making sales happen", the more reliable you are in saying X sales will happen in a time frame and X sales actually happen in that time frame, the more likely you will consider yourself reliable as well as be considered reliable by others.

What great news! Here is a way to measure and increase your ability to perform in any domain.

Takeaway:

In any domain or area (e.g. work, relationship with your wife, baseball, etc.), your performance in that domain or area is a function of your reliability in that domain or area. Your reliability is the percentage of times that you keep your promised outcomes in that domain or area.

BEING ACCOUNTABLE BUILDS UP RELIABILITY

The more accountable you are, the more reliable you become.

Accountability is simply accounting for promised outcomes.

Without promised outcomes, there is no accountability: no accountability is possible without promised outcomes.

With no accountability, promised outcomes (either from yourself or others) are meaningless and typically ineffectual. No accountability implies a lack of awareness of the status of your promised outcomes.

A very simple practice for accountability is as follows:

- In the moment that you make a promised outcome, you make sure that you have sufficient willingness to make it happen and access to resources to make the promised outcome happen e.g. do you have enough money and time and team resources to make the promised outcome happen?

- The moment that you realize that your promised outcome will not happen, you get into communication with the person(s) you made the promised outcome to – to modify the promised outcome as appropriate to fit current realities of resources and willingness to fulfill the promised outcome and accept consequences for the modification of your promised outcome.

- At the end of the promise period, you fully account for the promised outcome: DONE or NOT DONE and accept all consequences.

Notice:

You don't have to necessarily get a promised outcome done to fully be accountable.

That does not let you off the hook: it gives you flexibility, but not a reason to be slimy and keep making promised outcomes that you never intend to fulfill completely.

As you become a high performer and take on more complexity in your life, business or career, chances are great that you will miss making at least a few promised outcomes if not many promised outcomes. The practice of not accounting for these promised outcomes results in a clouding of the brain functions and the additional strain of trying to look good or keeping track of who to avoid or what to avoid so that you are not held to account – this can be a lot more work than being accountable. However, I find that being accountable does not require this kind of cost benefit analysis – just being accountable for the sake of choice, freedom and power is a powerful and effective way to be in life.

WHY IS ACCOUNTABILITY CRITICAL TO PERFORMANCE AND MAKING MORE TIME, MORE MONEY WITH LESS STRESS?

Accounting for your promised outcomes (implied or explicit promised outcomes) keeps the mind crystal clear. When you have unaccounted for promised outcomes, your mind tends to be clouded – often with worry, uncertainty or the experience of something incomplete for you or in your life.

When clients account for a promised outcome, I find that they experience clarity and freedom right away – even if the promised outcome is not fulfilled.

AWARENESS OF PROMISED OUTCOMES AND RELIABILITY -> PERFORMANCE

The first key to any change is awareness. The more aware you are of your current levels of willingness and tendencies to be accountable, the more likely you are to make future changes and transformation possible.

Get Into Action:

Make a list of all unaccounted for promised outcomes in your life: List out actions by each of these items that will have these promised outcomes be accounted for e.g. get into communication with the person you made the promised outcome to – to negotiate a resolution.

RELIABILITY = ULTIMATE MEASURE OF COMMITMENT

Over the long term, outcomes don't lie. Your true measure of your commitment to anything is in the outcomes that you produce over a reasonable timeframe. e.g. If you commit to loving your spouse and if you consistently fail to keep your agreements with your spouse, then your commitment is questionable.

Get into Action:

Identify the areas where you are having difficulty keeping your promised outcomes.

Rate your reliability in each of these areas: on a scale of 1-10 (10 being high reliability)

Similarly rate your commitment level for each area.

What did you learn from this exercise?

NOTES:

SCHEDULING INCREASES RELIABILITY

I have found in my coaching practice, that people increase their reliability when they schedule times (with an alarm set) to fulfill on the promised outcome.

This works because it reduces the overwhelm on the brain to remember the outcome. Most people rely on their memory when it comes to fulfilling on their outcomes – they rarely or never schedule times when they make a outcome.

This poor habit of trying to rely on your memory is costly in terms of your peace of mind, health, relationships and your financial success.

Takeaway:

If you are committed to keeping your promised outcomes, then schedule immediately every time you make a promised outcome to yourself or to someone else.

NOTES:

DECISION MAKING: WAYS TO CLARITY

There are two ways that I suggest to make it easier to clarify and make your decisions:

- Pros and Cons

- Risk and Return

PROS AND CONS

There is a tendency for people to procrastinate on making decisions. Often making a decision gets in the way of making more money in less time with less stress.

One way to make decisions is to list out your options or choices and then to weigh the pros and cons for each option.

Exercise:

- List out the decisions that you know you need to make

- For each decision, identify the options for resolving the decision

- For each option, list out the pros (benefits) and the cons (or the reasons not to do this option)

- Select the option that you commit to

- If you are still stuck in making a decision, look to see if something is out of integrity or if you have a conflict in your outcomes that is preventing making this decision clearly

RISK AND RETURN

In order to become more entrepreneur minded, you may have to assess risk and return in your life and work to make clear decisions.

Exercise:

- List out the decisions that you know you need to make

- For each decision, identify the options for resolving the decision

- For each option, list out the Risks and the Returns (Potential profit – monetarily or in terms of psychic satisfaction)

- Select the option that you commit to

- If you are still stuck in making a decision, look to see if something is out of integrity or if you have a conflict in your outcomes that is preventing making this decision clearly

Completion: Why You should be confident: The Art and Science of attaining mastery in becoming an Outcome Generator

To create more money, more time and less stress, there are clearly a number of practices to master.

Outcome Generators are people who know how to and actually are very reliable at producing outcomes.

Some characteristics:

- They are reliable at producing outcomes: when they say X happens by a certain time, X happens before that time.

- They are open to different ways of doing things, but are clear about certain basics (accountability, basic foundations of integrity, etc.)

- They have an infectious quality: other people want to and like being around them: this does not necessarily mean that they are extroverts – it means that people like being around them because of the reliability and certainty that they create in their outcomes and with other people.

When you take on higher levels of performance, accountability and responsibility, inevitably you are going to have to learn how to be an Outcome Generator.

You may know people who are Outcome Generators – they may make it seem very easy to do.

But becoming an Outcome Generator requires lots of practice.

Becoming a Master Outcome Generator will require lots of practice and a willingness to keep learning and fine tuning.

In the course of coaching and speaking to thousands of people, I have been fortunate to have worked with people who were already outcome generators or who were willing to learn and did become outcome generators.

In our survey interviews that we conduct with our very successful clients, we have found that when we ask them what they learned most in the coaching program, the response is invariably some form of the following: "Consistency and Practice".

When we examine their outcomes over the period of time, we can see occasional breakthrough up ticks in performance; but for the most part, the graph of progress indicates a slow but sure build.

Why do I share this with you?

Because I believe that you have the capacity to make yourself and your team or company successful and you don't have to rely on abstract philosophies or inspiration. I tell people that inspiration is for amateurs – real professionals learn to value and even enjoy the process of recovering from a failure, to take up the challenge again and to keep staying in the game until success hits. It is that level of dedication and distinction that separates the consistent players from the inconsistent ones.

There is nothing wrong with failure. There is nothing right about it either. A failure is a communication back to you to adjust and fine tune. That is all. There is no inherent judgment in a failure unless you speak the judgment.

If you treat the communication as a communication that you can respond to, you will be well served over time. If you ignore the communication, then you may be losing out on the best opportunity to learn and grow to become more consistent.

If you are the kind of person who tends to compare herself or himself to others, fret not. The success that you gain via the practices mentioned in this book are ones that will probably serve you for quite a long time as they are based on brain science and on observations of people who have been consistently successful.

"Life is like a snowball. The important thing is finding
wet snow and a really long hill"
Warren Buffett – Billionaire[xxxviii]

NEXT STEPS FOR YOU:

- Adopt and apply the practices in this book ASAP

- Start slow and pace yourself: remember mastery takes time – it takes time for your brain to make connections between what is said here, what you practice, your outcomes and the other complexities that make up your life and your business/profession

- Recommendation: ASAP: Hire a coach who will listen keenly to your style and be flexible with you in approach while being firm about focus on outcomes. Olympic athletes who are committed to mastery hire a coach; a coach can see things that you may not and point you in the direction to clear out the blind spots, keeping you focused on the outcomes and the fulfillment of your mission without compromising balance

- Commit to being a master in the distinctions contained in this book; this may take years to accomplish – but if you commit to being a master now, you may find yourself at least hitting some decent outcomes in the days and weeks and months that come

Sunil Bhaskaran

Coaching

I recommend using my coaching/training programs in conjunction with reading this book. You can use the book without coaching and still derive plenty of benefits - however coaching provides an additional dialogue and customization of these concepts to your particular circumstances, style and business.

Please refer to my website: www.CahayaMind.com for more information on coaching programs, our free reports on business performance, our blog and other useful tools and insights.

ABOUT SUNIL

Brain-Activated, Performance-Enhancement Specialist

Sunil Bhaskaran, a former engineer for many years, became very interested in Brain Science as a vehicle for helping business owners and corporate professionals enhance their focus, creativity, confidence and performance...to work smarter, not harder.

Mentor, Coach, Author & Speaker...

Having owned and run several businesses himself, Sunil speaks, trains and mentors from his own real-life experiences. Sunil began coaching and training people in 1989; and he has been in high demand as a mentor, private coach and keynote speaker for more than 20 years. His **"Brain Performance Program"** has made a profound difference in the bottom-line of thousands of business people worldwide. Additionally, Sunil has designed leadership, diversity, and accountability trainings for the corporate world at companies like Cisco, Comerica Bank, Compass Cares, to name a few.

Born and raised in Singapore, Sunil came to the US to study. He has degrees in Electrical Engineering and Computer Science from UC Irvine; and he worked as an engineer and an engineering manager for nine years. Sunil also had his own successful personal development radio show on KSCO, Santa Cruz: "Let's Talk Relationships" and was a radio personality, contributing his wit and humor to an ongoing weekly show. His first book, "The Forgiving Universe" (www.ForgivingUniverse.com) has been published and is available on Amazon. Sunil lives in the Santa Cruz area with his wife, Glenda.

Sunil Bhaskaran

"Finish each day and be done with it. You have done what you could.
Some blunders and absurdities no doubt crept in; forget them as soon
as you can. Tomorrow is a new day; begin it well and serenely and with
too high a spirit to be cumbered with your old nonsense."
- Ralph Waldo Emerson

ACKNOWLEDGEMENTS

- For my business partner, David Bookout – thank you for your creative and critical input – adding fire to the crucible leading to the selection of the best thoughts and ideas

- For my late father who taught me the value of patience and being consistent

- For my mother who taught me the value of discipline mixed with love

- For Lisa and her wonderful selection of graphics and colors to make a wonderful book cover

- For Evelyn and her fine work on our website

- For Sue and her patient and diligent work in keeping us all coordinated and sane

- For my wife …. No number of acknowledgements is sufficient to express my love

- For my family and communities – often unbeknownst to you, I had paid attention and learned from each and every one of you

- For my clients, I owe you a debt of gratitude – you learn from me as well as I learn from each and every one of you

- And last but not least, all the counselors, coaches and trainers who have worked with me either in a consultative role or as business partners – you made a huge difference

Thank you!
Sunil Bhaskaran

Sunil Bhaskaran

END NOTES: REFERENCES

(Endnotes)

[i]   NBC news 2007   http://www.nbcnews.com/id/20381678/#.URhsn2d5gdU

[ii]   "To Read or Not to Read. A question of National Consequence" by National Endowment for the Arts – Research Report #47

[iii] "Stress in America : Our Health at Risk" American Psychological Association: Jan 11th 2012

[iv]   I acknowledge Dr. Mihalyi Csikszentmihalyi, researcher in positive psychology and author of the book "Flow", for this distinction between pleasure and enjoyment

[v]   The brain is plastic. Neuroplascticity is an actual scientific term that means that the brain is able to make new and different connections all the time – even through old age (unless you have a severely damaged or diseased brain)

[vi]   An actual client whose name has been changed for client confidentiality reasons

[vii] Reference: Dunning-Kruger effect: People overestimate their abilities in all kinds of areas: http://en.wikipedia.org/wiki/Dunning%E2%80%93Kruger_effect

[viii] Reference: http://en.wikipedia.org/wiki/Mobile_phone: In the twenty years from 1990 to 2011, worldwide mobile phone subscriptions grew from 12.4 million to over 5.6 billion, penetrating the developing economies and reaching the bottom of the economic pyramid.

[ix]   Reference: "Hamlet's Blackberry" by William Powers – page 13

[x]   You may ask "Then how do I drive and eat a burger and pay attention to the radio at the same time?" These are tasks that are not in the category of day to day: they are also tasks that you have had a considerable amount of practice in (except of course when you first start driving). The practice over years of driving has enabled the skills and responsiveness of your driving to become more automatic: involving a different part of your brain (the basal ganglia) from the part of your brain usually used for day to day work (your prefrontal cortex). When it comes to day to day work, that work is typically handled by your prefrontal cortex: this part of the brain only allows for very limited task switching: i.e. it switches attention from one task to another sequentially – it does not allow for two tasks to be directed simultaneously – when you do a lot of task switching, a lot more energy and memory is used inefficiently.

[xi]   Reference: "Brain Rules" by John Medina – pages 86 to 87. Also read the studies on cell phone usage (multi tasking while driving) on these pages – you will probably never want to drive and use your cell phone at the same time again: not to mention doing your makeup or other activities while driving.

[xii] What is slowed down is not the entire brain but the prefrontal cortex – the part of the brain that is most engaged in day to day work

[xiii]   Reference: Ramsey, NF et al (2003) Neurophysiological factors in human information processing capacity Brain 127: 517 - 525

[xiv]   ADHD : Attention Deficit Hyperactivity Disorder – is a mental disorder and a neurobehavioral disorder characterized by either significant difficulties or inattention or hyperactivity and impulsiveness or the combination of the two. http://en.wikipedia.org/wiki/Attention_deficit_hyperactivity_disorder

[xv] "Flow – The psychology of optimal experience" by Dr. Mihalyi Csikszentmihalyi: Pg 6.

[xvi]   Reference: "Willpower" by Dr. Roy Baumeister and John Tierney: Dr. Roy Baumeister has researched willpower and similar topics extensively: http://en.wikipedia.org/wiki/Roy_Baumeister

[xvii]   Reference: "Willpower" by Dr. Roy Baumeister and John Tierney: page 44: "The glucose itself does not enter the brain, but it's converted into neurotransmitters, which are the chemicals that your brain cells use to send signals. If you ran out of neurotransmitters, you'd stop thinking"

[xviii]   Reference The Research of Dr. Roy Baumeister: especially on Decision Fatigue: One theory: What really happens is that the brain detects a decrease in glucose and assumes an alarming or dangerous situation is about to occur and shuts down prefrontal cortical functions as well as other functions in the brain and body to preserve energy: this shutting down of functions leads to reduced brain and will power. Refer to research on athletes by T.D. Noakes et al: The thinking is that fatigue in athletic efforts is similar to fatigue in typical brain or creative work:

   i.   Noakes, T.D., A. St Clair Gibson, and E.V. Lambert "From Catastrophe to Complexity: A Novel Model of Integrative Central Neural regulation of Effort and Fatigue During Exercise in Humans: Summary and Conclusions". British Journal of Sports Medicine 39 (2005): 120-24

   ii.   Noakes, T.D., J.E. Peltonen, and H.K. Rusko, "Evidence that a Central Governor Regulates Exercise Performance During Acute Hypoxia and Hyperoxia" the Journal of Experimental Biology 204 (2001): 3225-34

[xix]   This is mostly from anecdotal evidence – observations of clients over 22 years

[xx]   Research done by Dr. Roy Baumeister: http://en.wikipedia.org/wiki/Roy_Baumeister

[xxi]   http://en.wikipedia.org/wiki/Dopamine#Learning.2C_reinforcement.2C_and_reward-seeking_behavior

[xxii]   Research of Professor Wolfram Schultz : http://jn.physiology.org/content/80/1/1.short

[xxiii]   Rise of the Creative Class by Professor Richard Florida

[xxiv]   Some scientists refer to this as a hot or cold system: hot system is the system that responds in a 'negative' sense: e.g. fear and anxiety. Cold systems refer to the rational part of us (including the prefrontal cortex) – calm and objective

rationalization and analysis. Refer to Walter Mischel of Columbia University (Hot – Amygdala and Ventral Striatum and Cold systems - PFC).

xxv   Charlie Rose: Brain Science Series 1: www.CharlieRose.com

xxvi   Obviously there is no such thing as a King Bee, but I felt compelled to use this term so as not to exclude my male brothers from the very workable distinction that is expressed by "Queen Bee"

xxvii   D.S. Kirschenbaum, L.L. Humphrey, and S.D. Malett, "Specificity of Planning in Adult Self-Control: An Applied Investigation", Journal of Personality and Social Psychology 40 (1981): 941-50.

xviii   Page 71: "Willpower" by Roy F. Baumeister and John Tierney: Distal to proximal goals

xxix   Research by Professor Wolfram Schultz of Cambridge University

xxx   This was measured in the proportion of the project that they picked to do or in the actual number of accomplishments

xxxi   This makes sense if you consider that the PFC (prefrontal cortex) has a very low working memory: by most studies, it can handle about 7 items of memory at a time. Also studies by Yerkes-Dodson confirm this as well. http://en.wikipedia.org/wiki/Yerkes%E2%80%93Dodson_law. Also refer to our sections detailing willpower and glucose.

xxxii   From the work of Dr. Mihalyi Csikszentmihalyi: See references above pertaining to him

xxxiii   Refer to pg 56 of the book 'Subliminal – How Your Unconscious Mind Rules Your Behavior' by Leonard Mlodinow: the author describes how people with supposed good memories make inaccurate recalls of what happened in the past.

xxxiv   For a good more detailed and interesting reading on this, please refer to the book "Brain Rules" by Dr. John Medina

xxxv   Again, "Brain Rules" by Dr. John Medina gives a good summary of the research into sleep and sleep habits

xxxvi   For more reading on the RDA and to ascertain your RDA for water: http://en.wikipedia.org/wiki/Dietary_Reference_Intake

From: http://www.myfooddiary.com/resources/ask_the_expert/recommended_daily_water_intake.asp

"There are many different methods for calculating daily fluid requirements. However, a simple equation to help adults figure their fluid needs is that for every pound of body weight, you need about half an ounce of fluid intake per day. For instance, if you weigh 140 lbs., simply multiply 140 by .5 to estimate your daily fluid needs in ounces, then divide by eight to estimate your fluid needs in cups per day, rounding up to the nearest full cup. [example: 140 x .5 = 70 ounces; 70

ounces divided by 8 = 9 cups of fluid per day]" Note: The cup mentioned here is not a cooking cup measure: Be sure to use the correct measure of cup: typically an 8 ounce bottled water available in most stores will tell you how much a cup is. Pour this amount into your usual drinking cup to get an idea of how much you have to drink to maintain a healthy body – be prepared to be shocked and surprised at the amount. The good news is with practice, you can get yourself up to these seemingly large quantities of water drinking per day.

[xxxviii] Reference "The Snowball – Warren Buffett and the Business of Life" by Alice Schroeder – the biography of Warren Buffett – the billionaire.

www.ingramcontent.com/pod-product-compliance
Lightning Source LLC
Chambersburg PA
CBHW051334170526
45166CB00002B/815